UNASSIMILABLE

UNASSIMILABLE

An Asian Diasporic Manifesto for
the Twenty-First Century

BIANCA MABUTE-LOUIE

HARPER

An Imprint of HarperCollins*Publishers*

HarperCollins books may be purchased for educational, business, or sales promotional use. For information, please email the Special Markets Department at SPsales@harpercollins.com.

FIRST EDITION

Designed by Kyle O'Brien

Art by Bianca Mabute-Louie

Library of Congress Cataloging-in-Publication Data has been applied for.

ISBN 978-0-06-327762-5

24 25 26 27 28 LBC 5 4 3 2 1

For Popo, Yeye, and Bacbac

Author's Note

With the exception of quoted experts and public figures, I have changed the names and identifying characteristics of people I know to protect their privacy. The stories and conversations in this book reflect my memory of events. Others may recall shared experiences differently.

Contents

UNASSIMILABLE

Introduction

I grew up in San Gabriel Valley—also referred to as SGV or the 626—an ethnoburb in Los Angeles County where Asian immigrants go to never assimilate. Asian immigrants in the 1970s, initially mostly Chinese, built our own ethnic enclave, economy, and ecosystem in SGV. Chinese banks, Chinese grocery stores, Chinese-language schools on Saturday mornings for their ABC (American-born Chinese) children, and Chinese hair salons (because there are few things more frightening than the inability to communicate with your hairdresser and walking out of the salon with surprise bangs). I grew up with two Wing Hop Fung locations, each a ten-minute drive away from our one-story, three-bedroom home in the ethnoburb. Wing Hop Fung was where I fabricated stories in my head about my mom being a Chinese herb witch, as I watched her gather pungent, brightly colored seeds and plants to slow cook medicinal stews that would restore my yin and "undo the effects of all the fried chicken and pizza I ate at Jessica's birthday party last weekend." Dr. Lee, who provided psychiatry services in Mandarin, Cantonese, and Toisan, practiced down the street. Chinese Baptist Church held worship services, Sunday school, and weekly Bible study in English, Mandarin, and Cantonese around the corner. 99 Ranch, Quickly, and King Hua for the best dim sum outside of Hong Kong were all in our zip code. Across the street from King Hua was Costco, where they carried mooncakes, lap cheong, and dehydrated sea cucumber in bulk, because hoarding dehydrated sea cucumber in bulk is apparently the love language of immigrant dads. Everything we needed was in the ethnoburb.

My popo relocated from Hong Kong to join us in SGV when she was in her seventies. When she and her husband prepared to retire and settle down in Hong Kong, he instead decided to start a new family with a woman decades younger whom he'd had a secret affair with for almost ten years. Without any options and overwhelmed by shame, my popo left her home, her apartment where she raised three children with her ex-husband, and her mah-jongg group in Hong Kong to live with us in San Gabriel. She started over at seventy in a foreign place where she couldn't speak the language, didn't have any peers, and couldn't get around. She was isolated and heartbroken. With barely a kindergarten education, her life ambition was to become a wife and a mother. She loved flaunting how good she was at both roles. In true Cantonese matriarch fashion, she bragged incessantly to her social circles about her husband's and children's accomplishments. Now, with three adult children with families of their own, she was not needed as a mother, and no longer a wife. She had no purpose. Her ex-husband's affair decimated all status and belonging she held in their community. When I was a child, she would insist, "Your popo has become a useless nothing." It perplexed me because I never saw her that way.

But getting left by her husband wasn't her entire story.

With the safety net of the ethnoburb, she rebuilt. After living with us for a few years, she moved into her own one-bedroom apartment on Main Street in Alhambra, a city that neighbored San Gabriel at the heart of the ethnoburb. She walked to 85 Degrees everyday, where they rang a cowbell whenever fresh baos came out of the oven. She made friends with Cantonese neighbors in her building, and they started their own mah-jongg group where they would debrief the latest episode of whichever Cantonese drama that aired on TVB the previous night. She found a Cantonese church and got baptized. She never learned English, drove recklessly in the 99 Ranch parking lot, and didn't give a fuck. She may have confirmed a few stereotypes, but the ethnoburb saved her. She stayed unapologetically herself through the upheavals of divorce and displacement. In the safety net of SGV, she got her groove back.

Sometimes my mom would take my popo out of SGV to go window-shopping in Beverly Hills, and they would drag me along. As a child, Popo outside of the ethnoburb was a frightening, multisensory experience. She always brought her full self. She was large and in charge. She tried to bargain and make deals. In Cantonese. At Saks. They do not speak Cantonese there. They also do not tolerate haggling there. Her voice and presence were always loud, even and *especially* when we were the only Asians around. You don't speak Cantonese? Too bad and sit tight, because Popo is about to start her diatribe about her cheating ex-husband who you've never met before in a language you don't understand. 626 or 90210, my popo did not code switch. I, on the other hand, started my PhD in code switching when I was nine, after transferring to an uppity, predominantly White private school.

Popo outside of the ethnoburb was an unassimilable tornado that left me in the dust, embarrassed and flustered. Whiteness taught me to be ashamed of her behavior because Whiteness is actually terrified of people like my popo, coming out of the ethnic enclave and daring to assert herself into White spaces. When immigrants like my popo settle in a place like SGV en masse, White people are so afraid that they need to relocate. It's called White flight. It scares them when we collectively create our own belonging without participating in the traditional, time-honored process of assimilation. In ethnoburbs like SGV, White flight occurred because "too many" Asians like my popo arrived, bought up property, refused to acculturate, and made it our own. We disturb Whiteness and destabilize American respectability politics when we create and thrive in our own systems without them. The ethnoburb flourishes despite not assimilating. In fact, it flourishes *because* it doesn't assimilate.

My popo and the ethnoburb demonstrate that we can create our own power and belonging without learning English, participating in White institutions, and Americanizing. But it is a communal endeavor, one that requires everybody's imagination and care. Unassimilability is not an act of individualism; it is an interdependent community of popos finding each other, helping each other refill their prescriptions, and setting weekly dim sum dates so nobody gets too isolated. I question if my popo could have had her comeback tour if not for the Asian immigrants who came before her and with her, collectively creating their own sense of home in the diaspora through the ethnoburb.

As many early Asian immigrants to this country were barred from accessing White institutions, working together to build and protect the ethnic ecosystem was a matter of survival and necessity. Over a century later, unassimilability is the vision I witnessed among my popo and her friends in the ethnoburb, relying on each other in their collective insistence to thrive in their latter years, away from their homelands. Unassimilability is about cultivating our own social networks and daring to prosper in America without Whiteness. It is our ancestors and the elders creating home.

I GREW UP IN THE ETHNOBURB WITH EVERYTHING I NEEDED, AND still, the ethnoburb was limited. The goal my parents communicated to me was to attend predominantly White schools, get admitted into their universities, and work stable jobs in their institutions. As the ethnoburb created resources in the forms of shadow education and SAT prep catered to second-generation youth to achieve these goals, so began my laboring for validation from Whiteness. I suppose everything worked out as planned. I got initiated into PWI after PWI (Predominantly White Institutions), until I was surrounded by Whiteness and suddenly embarrassed of the unapologetically Asian ethnoburb that got me there. I was nine when I started at my first PWI and, almost overnight, began pretending I didn't understand Chinese, lying to my White peers about where I lived, and trying to throw tantrums to get out of Chinese school (it never worked because I was too afraid of my mom to follow through). In its unassimilability, the ethnoburb ironically gave me the support and resources to approach adjacency to Whiteness and resent where I came from. Unlike my popo, I was easily and eagerly assimilable.

Taking Ethnic Studies a decade later helped me critically interrogate and reject the compulsory assimilation of growing up in America (even in the ethnoburb), and I've mostly dropped the facade. I clumsily persevere through as much Cantonese as I can in my biweekly calls to my parents, even though I speak like a first grader. I visit Bellaire, the Asian ethnoburb in Houston, foraging for goji berries, dried dates, and white fungus at 99 Ranch and H Mart to try to become my own Chinese herb witch. I teach and write about Asian American identity. And still, at my current PWI, where I'm completing my doctoral degree, I catch myself continually longing. More nods of approval, more publications, more awards, more proximity, more validation, more recognition, from them. I tell myself it's not at all about Whiteness, but about wanting to succeed in a system never made for me. But ultimately, they are the ones who continually define success, and I'm left wondering when it will be enough, and when I will be enough.

The compulsion and pressure to assimilate are nothing new. For many, assimilation has been a survival mechanism. Among early Chinese immigrants in the US, the assimilability versus unassimilability binary was a weaponizing concept. As the early Chinese population in San Francisco expanded in the mid-1800s, so did White anxieties about Chinese immigrants taking gold, jobs, and resources. The yellow peril stereotype positioned Chinese immigrants, and by extension all Asians, as a dangerously unassimilable, heathen, and diseased threat to US society. In contrast to early European immigrants, who would eventually become White through acculturation and render their ethnic ties relatively inconsequential, Asian immigrants could never assimilate. Our foreignness would always be visible and consequential, threatening Whiteness, and thereby a barrier to our own citizenship.

The unassimilable yellow peril stereotype justified anti-Asian laws and White supremacist violence that disadvantaged and terrorized early Chinese immigrant communities. The 1850 foreign miner's tax, for example, stipulated that no foreigners could work his mining claim unless he paid a monthly license fee in gold dust, a fee arbitrarily increased by California over the next few years. The fee was only applied to Chinese and Latino miners, not European miners, and corruptly enforced by collectors who pocketed money and physically assaulted our communities. With Latinos, our safety and security were at the whim of Whiteness. Falling on the unassimilable side of the binary had dire and material consequences on our communities, and I often wonder how this memory of violent exclusion stays embodied within and among us, several generations later. Perhaps this is why I find myself achieving my aspirations yet inadvertently still striving for the PWI approval. Or maybe I'm desperate to find some intergenerational connective tissue to my ancestors to make me feel more at ease about my neurosis in graduate school.

In the chance that it is at least partially intergenerational, then unassimilability and resistance must also run in me. Despite the racial violence and hostility, Chinese immigrants in San Francisco still cultivated their own ethnic enclave with Chinese grocery stores, newspapers, and businesses. My paternal great-grandfather played an integral role in developing early San Francisco Chinatown, importing goods from South China to supply grocers. He and his brothers managed the transport and sales of dried sausage, mushrooms, rice, and herbs. I like to imagine him as the community lap cheong dealer, hustling on Kearny Street to offer a taste of home to the diaspora while securing remittances to send back to his family. At a time when Chinese immigrants were excluded from White neighborhoods and institutions, he helped San Francisco's historic Chinatown grow its own.

To pursue this opportunity, my great-grandfather left my great-grandmother, two daughters, and adopted son (my grandfather) in Hong Kong. Financial constraints made it impossible for him to travel back to see his family. Even if he'd had the resources, immigration restrictions made it risky for him to leave and enter back into the US without being detained on Angel Island. There was no such thing as family reunification. The country wanted Asian labor, not Asian families, communities, or humanity. The Page Act of 1875 banned all Chinese women from entering the US on the assumption that they were sexually immoral prostitutes, making the early Chinese immigrant community a bachelor society. But who are we without our kin? In the diaspora, my great-grandfather created chosen family in Chinatown through associations, formed around family names and province of origin. Associations served as political and social support systems to newcomers, helping meet basic needs of the community and representing a unified voice to fight discriminatory legislative processes.

As my great-grandfather organized with other early Chinese immigrants to build a defensive ecosystem, Whites felt threatened and doubled down on the yellow peril stereotype through legislative efforts. In April 1852, California governor John Bigler called for an exclusionary law to bar future Chinese immigrants, representing the first declaration of anti-Chinese sentiment by a public official.[1] Media soon swiveled to bolster Bigler's virulently racist position. By 1853, the *San Francisco Daily Alta California* published,

> [The Chinese were] morally a far worse class to have among us than the negro. . . . They are not of that kin that Americans can ever associate or sympathize with. They are not of our people and never will be, though they remain here forever. . . . They do not mix with our people, and it is undesirable that they should, for nothing but degradation can result to us from the contact. . . . They can never become like us.

A SERIES OF EXCLUSION LAWS CODIFIED ASIANS AS RACIALLY unassimilable and ineligible for citizenship, with the Chinese Exclusion Act remaining in US law from 1882 until 1943. My great-grandfather died of lung cancer right after the Chinese Exclusion Act was lifted, never getting the chance to return home and reunite with his family.

Unassimilability assumes Asians pose a racial danger to American society, and we are especially threatening when we are organized and able to provide for ourselves. Unlike

assimilable European immigrants of the time, who also cultivated their own ethnic enclaves, our undeniable foreignness
inherently endangered the racial purity of this country. These
stereotypes returned with antagonistic US-China geopolitical
relations and inflammatory political rhetoric during COVID-19
(e.g., "China virus"). All it takes is war or disease to resurrect
violent, racist narratives of Asian Americans and Chinatowns
as perpetually foreign, diseased, and unassimilable. We are
easily at the whim of Whiteness, and the impulse to assimilate
and cooperate is especially seductive in times of crisis.

At the onset of anti-Asian racism from the COVID-19
pandemic, 2020 Democratic Party presidential primaries
candidate Andrew Yang called for Asian Americans to respond to the rise in discriminatory incidents by proving our
"Americanness." Yang called on us to wear red, white, and
blue; be civically engaged; and proudly show the world that
"we are Americans." He compared the moment to World
War II, when large numbers of Japanese Americans volunteered for military duty to prove their patriotism.[2] But
Japanese American soldiers giving their lives to the military-
industrial complex to prove their Americanness did not keep
them safe. One hundred twenty thousand Japanese Americans were still violently surveilled, incarcerated, and denied
basic citizenship rights because they were deemed dangerous
and unassimilable. They were still dehumanized.

Asian American cultural campaigns also emerged during
the pandemic with slogans like "I'm from here." These messages not only erase North American Indigenous peoples, who
are the only ones "from here," but are ineffective in keeping
us safe. After Yang published his op-ed, anti-Asian attacks

increased by 150 percent in major cities throughout the pandemic.³ A targeted White supremacist shooting at a spa in Atlanta murdered six Asian women. One in five Asian Americans who had experienced racism displayed symptoms of racial trauma.⁴ Asian Americans who had experienced racism were more stressed by anti-Asian hate than the pandemic itself.⁵ Throughout history and more recently, laboring to prove our citizenship and belonging does not secure our safety in this country. Asserting our Americanness does not actually protect, save, or legitimate us.

At the cornerstone of exclusion is the violent binary between assimilable and unassimilable, deserving and undeserving, good and bad. The "model minority" stereotype, for example, positions East Asians as the "good, hardworking, and law-abiding" minority, pitting us against Black and Brown communities, who are commonly stereotyped as "lazy" or "criminal." In the immigrant rights movement of the 2010s, DREAMers were deemed as the "good immigrants" because they were educated, and received temporary protection from deportation because of Deferred Action for Childhood Arrivals (DACA). Immigrants working in domestic, agricultural, or construction labor, on the other hand, were supposedly "stealing jobs and not paying taxes" (both of which are untrue), making them "undeserving" and deportable. Feminist abolitionist organizers like Survived & Punished and Mariame Kaba have shown us the lengths our society and the criminal justice system go to separate the "good" sexual assault and domestic violence victims from "bad" ones. "Bad" victims are frequently Black women criminalized and punished for protecting themselves and their families against abusers. "Good" victims, on the other hand, are the innocent White women who go missing on true-crime shows, deserving of our sympathy and protection.

These binaries, covertly and overtly weaponized against all of us, are rooted in what Black feminist author bell hooks defines and critiques as imperialist White supremacist capitalist heteropatriarchy. hooks explains the ways imperialism, capitalism, racism, heterosexism, and patriarchy work together to oppress in overlapping and distinctive ways (much like Kimberlé Crenshaw's term "intersectionality"). The norms constructed by these systems facilitate a politic of disposability, protecting those perceived as deserving and valuable and inflicting violence on those who are deemed disposable. The US as an empire legislates this politic of disposability, from local to national to international levels. While we are affected by oppression in distinct ways depending on who we are, the through line is imperialist White supremacist capitalist heteropatriarchy, which hooks insisted on naming over and over again so we can eradicate it. We are often pitted against one another by imperialist White supremacist capitalist heteropatriarchy, as many of us feel coerced to assimilate and cooperate with Whiteness for the myth of survival and security. The Asian ethnoburb, for example, is seduced to distance itself from Blackness, while I am pulled to disaffiliate from my own Asianness, all to be perceived by Whiteness as deserving of belonging and protection.

For Asian Americans, assimilation into Whiteness and cooperation with the US as a nation state and an empire are not only about surviving the yellow peril stereotype and its violent consequences but about legal and social status. During World War II, Chinese Americans tried to position ourselves as the "good Asians" by disavowing Japanese Americans, who were scapegoated for the attacks on Pearl Harbor and labeled as the "foreign enemy" of the time. In a historic moment that could have inspired Asian pan-ethnic solidarity over shared experiences of stereotyping and discrimination, Chinese Americans chose to prove loyalty to the state instead of to other Asian Americans. Aligning with the US was especially consequential for our legal status at this time, with the importance of China as an ally in America's war against Japan leading to the repeal of the Chinese Exclusion Act. Pan-Asian group solidarity held minimal meaning against the possibility of legal inclusion into the US empire.

Of course, there have also always been movements of resistance. There were Chinese Americans who stood in solidarity with Japanese Americans during World War II. And while Yang lauded the Japanese Americans volunteering for military service, he neglected to mention the No-No Boys, a group of twelve thousand Japanese Americans who refused to show allegiance to and fight for a government that stripped away their civil rights and incarcerated them without cause. The No-No Boys received their name by answering "no" to two questions on a questionnaire given to Japanese Americans in the incarceration camps. Question number 27 asked, "Are you willing to serve in the armed forces of the United States on combat duty, wherever ordered?" and question number 28 asked, "Will you swear unqualified allegiances to the United States of America and faithfully defend the United States from any or all attack by foreign or domestic forces, and forswear any form of allegiance or obedience to the Japanese emperor, or other foreign government, power or organization?"

Outraged that the US demanded that they vow loyalty to the country after flagrantly violating their civil liberties and separating them from their families, the No-No Boys refused to enlist in the armed forces and participate in the US war machine. As essayists Gary Tachiyama and Roland Kotani explained, "[The No-No Boys] were castigated by the Japanese American community and the broader public as being disloyal traitors to the United States."[6] The No-No Boys suffered and lost immensely as a result of their defiance. The US transferred them to a War Relocation Authority segregation center established as a kind of brutal penal colony at Tule Lake to punish them.

While there have always been movements resisting the US empire, the pressures to assimilate persist. Some of us bravely risk everything to protest America's hypocrisies, and still others are ashamed of our resistance and would rather we quietly cooperate. The ways we are racialized by this country are unstable and reactive to geopolitics, so our racial politics in response are also slippery and precarious. More often than not, we are inconsistent and cacophonous in how we respond. As a collective, we simultaneously refuse and embolden the violence of the US empire.

Since the end of World War II, proving our allegiance to this country also became entangled with the model minority myth, strengthening the undercurrent toward assimilation. Asserting that Asian Americans are loyal, quiet, and good workers helped advocate for social inclusion and replace the yellow peril stereotype. We were no longer unassimilable and dangerous. Instead of threatening to take over and disrupt the racial order, we would now have the chance to cooperate and fortify it. Some of us, mostly East Asians, could work hard and shut up in exchange for conditional belonging and material security. We could get close to the protection of Whiteness.

The subtext beneath the model minority myth was "If Asians can get in line and succeed, why can't everybody else?" Journalists, politicians, and sociologists weaponized this rhetoric as fodder to strip away welfare and social services, pull back on civil rights wins like affirmative action, and delegitimize claims of ongoing systemic racism. The simplified, flattened case of Asian American "success" is continually used as an ideological weapon against Black and Latino communities who face significant and distinct systemic barriers. The model minority myth is a convenient anti-Black framework to explain racial inequality as a problem of individuals and ethnic cultures, not ideologies, policies, or institutions. And how many of us actually internalize this narrative, believing minorities who struggle simply have a poor work ethic? In fact, how many of us actually rely on positioning ourselves against Blackness in order to secure our own sense of worthiness in this country?

Through these racial dynamics, historian Ellen Wu argues, "Asian Americans' place in the racial landscape went from being 'definitively not White' to 'definitively not Black.'" By distancing from Blackness and aligning with the political goals of the US empire, many of us managed to not just survive the yellow peril stereotype but to find supposed social belonging in the US racial landscape. But this belonging always depended on our agreeability with Whiteness. We grew acceptable to the White gaze on the assumption that we would never threaten existing White political and institutional dominance. We became conditionally assimilable and maybe even respectable, as long as there isn't a war or a pandemic. This belonging relied on us imposing these ideologies on one another, policing members of our own community for not learning English, working low-wage menial jobs, and refusing to acculturate. We ostracize those among us who threaten our own assimilation.

I CERTAINLY *WANTED* TO REPUDIATE MY POPO WHEN SHE WAS yelling in Cantonese at Saks, but just as she could not be assimilated, she could not be corrected, certainly not by me. So instead, I stayed hidden in the clothing racks lest a White person saw me and associated us together. Popo aggressively threatened my compulsion to blend in and belong, but she was onto something. Proving our Americanness hasn't saved us. Being the "good minority" has us trapped in a liminal state between belonging and exclusion, where our rights of citizenship are conditional. So what if we, like my popo, refused to assimilate and cooperate? What if we dared to act large and in charge in spaces that expect us to shrink and contort ourselves to be palatable to Whiteness? What are the political possibilities of Asians in America who refuse to belong here and participate in this charade? What if we leaned into our *peril* as the fastest-growing electorate, and actively positioned ourselves as an unassimilable danger to Whiteness? The state wants our labor, but never our full humanity. So instead of trying to prove our loyalty to the state, what if we cultivated belonging with one another and practiced disloyalty to this country?

When enough of us refuse to assimilate and cooperate, we pose a threat to established racial hierarchies and we rewrite racial narratives. Like the ethnoburb, we threaten Whiteness when we don't assimilate. We turn the model minority myth on its head, refusing to be manipulated as the "good immigrants" who quietly give our labor to this country without threatening the status quo. We become rebellious. We become visible. We destabilize White supremacist hierarchies and narratives that depend on our silence and weaponize us against Blackness.

Unassimilability is a proposition to refuse to belong here altogether, together. It is a distinctly Asian American politic of refusal that rejects acceptance by the US empire as aspirational. Unassimilability frees us to define ourselves, our belonging, and our power independent of Whiteness. Unassimilability, when exercised collectively, is our weapon and hope against the violence of the US. Moving beyond the model minority myth, unassimilability is less about proving ourselves to Whiteness, and more about holding it accountable while divesting from it altogether. As evidenced by the COVID-19 wave of anti-Asian hatred, no amount of cooperation and "success" in the US can protect us from the arbitrary violence of how Whiteness perceives us. Thus, unassimilability is a liberatory paradigm, inviting us to align with one another, rather than with this country.

Throughout this book, I explore how unassimilability is expressed, suppressed, and negotiated in different sites of Asian diasporic life in America. I search for new names and language to clarify who we are and who we can be in this historic moment of social movements and revolutions. Octavia Butler wrote, "There's nothing new under the sun, but there are new suns." In our refusal of the US empire, I reconsider

the term "Asian American" and look for new suns. Historically, "Asian American" was an anti-racist, anti-imperialist,
and anti-capitalist political identity coined by UC Berkeley
graduate students Emma Gee and Yuji Ichioka during the
Asian American movement in the late 1960s. It has since
been reduced by the mainstream to politics of inclusion and
representation. I am ambivalent about the term's capacity to
hold our diverse experiences together and pessimistic about
its political utility at this current moment. Instead of anxiously
guarding the "American" part of these hyphenated identities,
what if we disavowed America and owned our diasporic sense
of racial placelessness? Being part of the Asian Diaspora is to
not have a place because of Western imperialism, Orientalism, and capitalism. Instead of trying to claim a place in this
genocidal, anti-Black fallacy of a country, what if we created
belonging in the diaspora by claiming one another? I propose
Asian Diaspora as an expansive political identity, one that
rejects belonging in America and centers the constellation of
Asian diasporic experiences, relationships, and resistance.

Both assimilability and unassimilability have cost me.
There is a price to pay for each paradigm. And yet, I struggle
toward unassimilability, even while assimilation is more convenient, comfortable, and safe. I find unassimilability is worth
whatever losses I accrue, because orienting myself away from
Whiteness and the US empire unlocks political imagination
to create a new collective identity with diasporic co-strugglers
against imperialist White supremacist capitalist heteropatriarchy. While assimilation may appear seductive, I've witnessed
the violence of the US—from Ferguson to Mauna Kea to Gaza

to all the sacred lands and people the US has bombed and colonized—and I refuse to pledge allegiance.

In *Minor Feelings*, Cathy Park Hong writes, "The paint on the Asian American label has not dried." Hong uses this metaphor to describe the unfinished and mercurial nature of Asian American as a political identity. Indeed, we are unfastened and paradoxical, simultaneously contracting and expanding in response to racial trauma, geopolitics, demographic changes, and social movements. We oscillate between assimilation and resistance. In our ongoing and often contradictory states, unassimilability is our effort to keep painting the portrait toward revolutionary politics and capacious solidarity. While the process is unwieldy and clumsy, radical political identity is an urgent aspiration and necessary endeavor. As the State reveals itself to be increasingly useless, violent, and hypocritical, daring to assert our unassimilability grounds us in ourselves, each other, and our collective power. Following my popo's lead, may we refuse to belong here, together.

(UN)AMERICAN BY BIRTH

TO DO IN TOISAN

kiss my wife

meet my son

help family business

honor ancestors

drink with buddies

hug my parents

1895, after WKA's trip, upon return to San Francisco

GO BACK TO WHERE YOU CAME FROM

JOHN H. WISE immigrant processing

I'm from here

I ORDER YOU TO RETURN TO CHINA

WKA was denied entry and detained for five months, unable to return to his home in San Francisco

John H. Wise attempted to apply discriminatory exclusion laws as broadly as possible

WISE

Self-described "zealous opponent" of Chinese immigration

Not to be mistaken with...

Vowed to end birthright citizenship for children of undocumented immigrants

TRUMP

Criminalized people TRANSPORTING undocumented immigrants

ABBOTT

WKA and his lawyers challenged the decision in court, arguing that he had a right to be admitted under the fourteenth amendment

"All persons born or naturalized in the U.S. are citizens of the U.S."

14th Amendment

White	Eligible
Native American	Ineligible
Black	Eligible on paper, not in practice
Asian	TBD

"Legally the WKA affair forced the Court to determine whether nonwhites born in the U.S. would be entitled citizenship on the same basis as applied to whites or be relegated to a permanent foreign underclass."
Iris Chang, author of *The Chinese in America*

In the landmark decision of US vs. Wong Kim Ark, the Supreme Court voted in favor of Wong, affirming that all persons born in the US, regardless of race, are entitled to citizenship and its rights, even if their parents are ineligible for naturalization.

AMERICAN BY BIRTH
Name *Wong Kim Ark*
Age *44*   Height *5 ft 6 1/4 in*
Occupation *cook, San Francisco*
Physical marks and peculariaties *scar on right temple*
Issued at the port *San Francisco, Cal* this *11th* day of *November 1914*

Despite the ruling, Wong and other Chinese Americans were treated as unequal citizens and forced to carry identification at all times as proof of legal residence.

Today

We should be grateful to be born in America and have our rights and citizenship protected. It used to be so much harder!

But what does citizenship mean to us today?

AMERICAN BY BIRTH
Assimilation instead of detainment,
A dream built on genocide and enslavement.
Integration into an economy,
That funds the US war machine.
Citizenship is a privilege,
Citizenship is a contradiction.
Citizenship is security,
Citizenship is fiction.

1
The Ethnoburb

I was back in San Gabriel Valley the summer after I graduated college, visiting the used bookstore at the San Marino library, in the more uppity part of SGV. I overheard an employee, a White woman in her seventies, proclaiming to a younger White woman, "My ancestors were immigrants too, but they assimilated. Unlike them—they come over, take over, don't even bother learning the language." She glanced at me and then back at her conversation partner. "San Marino didn't used to be like this. They're everywhere now." She spoke of the influx of families like mine like an unsettling pest invasion, infiltrating her spaces and disturbing her American suburb. In his book *Resisting Change in Suburbia: Asian Immigrants and Frontier Nostalgia in L.A.*, historian James Zarsadiaz writes that White folks' reactions to the demographic changes in San Gabriel Valley commonly ranged from dissatisfaction to outrage, the latter exemplified by this bookshop employee. Growing numbers of unassimilated Asian immigrants in the traditionally White suburb reflected the larger, changing contemporary world where White people no longer felt centered. The entire "adult" generation of my family in the US are immigrants; my cousins and I were the first to be born here. With the SGV ethnoburb as their entry point, they had minimal need or desire to assimilate. They learned the language, but spoke it rarely and clumsily and didn't seem to care. They ate, spoke, and breathed in Cantonese, and I was both embarrassed and protective of them. I wanted to shout in the bookstore, "We're not like that!" while I very well knew that we were, indeed, like that. My older family members felt no urgency to contort themselves for the White gaze, and I simultaneously admired and feared for them. I loved that they cared so little about acceptance from Whiteness, yet was terrified that they—and by extension I—would be ridiculed or punished for it. My parents and I often heard resentful, nativist comments like these from the diminishing minority of older White residents in San Gabriel Valley, and my mom always told me to ignore them. "There go those lo bak gwei again!" she would exclaim, using the derogatory term for White people in Cantonese, which literally translated into "old white ghosts," and then proceed to laugh hysterically.

Unlike my carefree mother, I froze in humiliation at that moment. Humiliation that this older White woman spoke the truth about our unassimilability, and framed it as a menace. Humiliation that I have thought similar sentiments about my family, and worried more about agreeing with and appeasing White discomfort than defending our own dignity. Humiliation that she stopped to acknowledge me before she continued her diatribe and I said nothing. I tried to file a complaint about her to the librarian. Somehow I thought the librarian would be the authority on microaggressions. But she just replied, "Oh yeah, she's been here forever. Nothing we can do."

FROM THE BEGINNING OF WORLD WAR II UNTIL 1960, MONTEREY Park, a neighboring city to San Marino and the origin of San Gabriel Valley as an ethnoburb, prospered as one of the most affordable White suburban communities. The wartime economy brought transplants from across the country to Southern California, and Monterey Park became an emerging site of comfortable single-family homes and manicured green lawns. Postwar Monterey Park remained predominantly White, but began to draw upwardly mobile Mexican, Japanese, and Chinese Americans from different ethnic enclaves around Los Angeles, including East Los Angeles, the Westside, and Chinatown.[1] In a time of charged debate and political struggle around race, segregation, and housing rights in California and across the nation, Asian Americans and Mexican Americans approached home buying in Monterey Park cautiously by gathering intel from intra-ethnic networks and assessing the attitudes of local real estate agents.

It helped that many Asian Americans and Mexican Americans looking to buy homes in Monterey Park were second- or third-generation immigrants: educated, acculturated, and relocating from LA's urban ethnic enclaves to pursue the dream of an upwardly mobile suburban life. Their integration—having assimilated into the American "melting pot" and holding relatively loose ties to their home countries and cultures compared to their first-generation predecessors—was relatively smooth.

Because they had social and financial capital and were few enough in numbers, they were not perceived as threatening to existing White political, institutional, and cultural dominance in Monterey Park. However, many of them still experienced racial discrimination at the time, pointing to the ways racism continued to define their increasingly integrated social worlds.

As Asian Americans and Mexican Americans gained relative acceptance from Monterey Park as a traditionally all-White suburb, Black Americans continued to face overt and violent resistance to home buying and integration. Geographer Wendy Cheng notes in her book *The Changs Next Door to the Díazes: Remapping Race in Suburban California* that anti-Black racism allowed Asian American and Mexican Americans to purchase homes and settle in Monterey Park, while Black Angelenos were continually hypersegregated in South Central Los Angeles and precluded from home buying in the suburbs. According to race scholars Eduardo Bonilla-Silva and Claire Jean Kim, racial hierarchy manipulates and positions Asian Americans and Mexican Americans "above" Black Americans and "below" Whites. This looked like White suburban residents going to great lengths to exclude Black Americans from moving in, while slowly (and begrudgingly) allowing Asian Americans and Mexican Americans to take up residence. In 1960, Whites made up 85.6 percent of Monterey Park, with Latinos at 11.6 percent, Asian Americans at 2.8 percent, and Black Americans at 0.04 percent. By 1970, Monterey Park became the first ethnically diverse middle-class suburb in the country, with Whites holding a majority at 50.5 percent, Latinos at 34 percent, Asian Americans at 15.3 percent, and Black Americans hovering at 0.2 percent.[2]

Growing up in San Gabriel Valley, I recall a distinct non-White identity rooted in the predominantly Asian and Latino middle-class suburban context. It was common to see Asian and Latino immigrants working, living, and existing together, crossing racial, cultural, and linguistic boundaries in everyday sites of work and school. However, in our ecosystem, where White people were peripheral, the racial hierarchies and politics created by Whiteness still permeated. I remember one Black student in preschool, and none in my elementary school. I witnessed rigid boundaries between us and Latinos in our neighborhood, and stereotypes of Black and Latino criminality and laziness permeated my family and the Chinese American community. We often bought into and reified racist, anti-Black, and anti-Latino racial frames to secure our own place as Asian Americans, which manifested in our day-to-day interracial relations and cultivated fear and resentment among Asian Americans toward Black and Brown communities. The racial hierarchy of the national context, which positions East Asians proximate to Whiteness vis-à-vis the model minority myth, infiltrated our local context. We didn't need White people in our ethnoburb to participate in the divide-and-conquer racial politics of Whiteness.

THROUGH THE 1970S AND '80S, MONTEREY PARK OFFICIALLY and dramatically transformed from its traditional White suburban image into an immigrant suburb with an Asian majority and a particularly visible presence of foreign-born Chinese residents. In 1950, there were fewer than ten Chinese residents in Monterey Park. That number jumped to 346 in 1960 and increased by 536 percent to 2,200 in 1970. We became the majority in 1990, with Asians at 57.5 percent (out of which 36.2 percent were Chinese). As of 2010, almost two-thirds of Monterey Park and its surrounding suburbs, Rosemead, Alhambra, and San Gabriel, were Asian American, and three in four residents were foreign-born. The "Chinese Golden Triangle" also emerged in East San Gabriel Valley in Rowland Heights, Walnut, and Diamond Bar, where there were 1,869 Chinese businesses in 1996, a number that remarkably rose to 4,683 by 2010.[3]

The 1943 repeal of the Chinese Exclusion Act, along with the passage of the Immigration and Nationality Act of 1965 (Hart-Celler Act), opened up unprecedented immigration opportunities for Asian immigrants and explain much of the demographic changes. In *The Making of Asian America*, historian Erika Lee writes, "[T]he majority of new arrivals come to join family already here and bring a different set of educational and professional skills than earlier immigrants."[4] Recent immigration laws have continued in the same trend, with the 1990 Immigration Act facilitating the flow of highly educated "guest workers" with temporary H-1B visas, most frequently utilized by high-skilled Asian workers in the high-tech sector.* Among them, professional Chinese immigrant workers include English-speaking scientists, real estate moguls, entrepreneurs, and white-collar elites. Immigration reforms in 1965 and 1990 created preferential categories based on family reunification

---

* In 2011, Asian immigrants received nearly 75 percent of all H-1B visas set aside for "highly skilled" immigrant workers.

and professional skills, and professional Chinese immigrants in Monterey Park took advantage of these liberalized immigration reforms to sponsor relatives and to create supportive networks for new arrivals.

In addition to more professional Asian immigrants, the end of American imperialist wars in the 1970s brought an influx of Vietnamese and other Southeast Asian refugees to the US. They resettled in ethnoburbs and Chinatowns, diversifying the demographic composition of the primarily working-class Cantonese- and Mandarin-speaking community to one that was socioeconomically heterogeneous as well as Vietnamese, Cambodian, Cantonese, and Mandarin. Further, many "low-skilled" and undocumented Asian immigrants were drawn to the ethnoburb because of job opportunities associated with the expanding ethnic economy and housing opportunities with family and friends. A growing number of Asian immigrants had minimal education and worked as waiters, domestic workers, garment workers, cooks, and laundrymen. An estimated 150,000 Chinese immigrants entered without documentation in the 1990s, and undocumented Asian immigrants made up a significant proportion (10–11 percent) of the total number of 11 million undocumented immigrant population in the US from 2000–2010. Undocumented Chinese immigrants working menial jobs were vulnerable to exploitation by more established Chinese residents. Even today, their wages are quickly depleted to pay back debts to smugglers and to send remittances home. Asians began to represent both extremes of educational and class spectrums, and the Chinese American population in particular continues to overrepresent both sides of the socioeconomic ladder.[5]

Asian immigrants arriving as educated professionals with financial resources, refugees displaced by American imperialism, and working-class and undocumented immigrants redefined Monterey Park as a socioeconomically diverse Asian ethnic enclave in the suburbs. Monterey Park was especially attractive given its proximity to Chinatown, relatively cheap land, and auspicious feng shui, with its hills considered to bring good luck.[6] Chain migration and rumors of economic opportunities in the ethnoburb facilitated the recruitment of additional Asian immigrants to Monterey Park and its surrounding communities. The Asian community in Monterey Park suddenly became highly diverse, especially in political histories, immigration backgrounds, and socioeconomic status. This heterogeneity reflected the broader emergence of a new, exceptionally diversified Asian America across the country.

Such development produced a hidden suburban inequality and socioeconomic fragmentation among Asian immigrants in Monterey Park, and later, in other ethnoburbs like Alhambra, El Monte, and Arcadia—all suburbs that make up the San Gabriel Valley. Much of the ethnic enclave and ethnoburb economies have been dependent on a vulnerable labor force that includes "low-skilled" Asian and Latino workers, many of whom are undocumented.[7] The proliferation of the ethnic economy in ethnoburbs produced conditions similar to old urban Chinatowns, with informal work, proletarianization of labor, and lack of bounded solidarity and trust among co-ethnics.

My parents emigrated from Hong Kong to the US as a result of the 1965 Hart-Celler Act, and were part of the momentous demographic shift of "Asians moving in" to Monterey

Park. They didn't know each other in Hong Kong but both ended up in Monterey Park because of chain migration: they heard rumors from friends that "there are a lot of Chinese people there." (I too am curious about and will go to places "with a lot of Chinese people there," because that usually means the food is good.) Unlike many of their Hart-Celler peers, however, they did not come with H-1B visas or formal education. My dad came from Hong Kong with his brothers as a high schooler on a tourist visa, and overstayed to continue his education. He would live undocumented for several years. When I ask him about what high school in Monterey Park was like in the 1970s, his stories are a mix of chaos, desperation, and adventure, embodied through his *Saturday Night Fever* perm. He and his brothers were three out of five Asians at a predominantly Mexican American school. He adjusted to school quickly and got along well with peers, but only because he got into multiple fights on his first day. He proudly boasts that he came onto the scene with fists up to communicate to his new peers "not to mess with him." He's watched too many Bruce Lee films.

My dad and uncles talk about "running buck wild" during these years without adult supervision. They rented an apartment, lived off of instant ramen, and smoked way too much weed (a fact that my dad will only admit when my mom isn't around). My dad and his brothers took care of one another and drove one another crazy. Without other familial support, they begrudgingly yet faithfully showed up for each other's brawls, milestones, and high school graduations. I imagine the three of them, with their chaos perms, causing a ruckus during the most inappropriate times, as they still do today. During these early, unsupervised years in Monterey Park, more and more Chinese immigrants like them began moving into their neighborhood. Consequently, White and second- and third-generation Asian American residents who had settled before the influx of new Chinese immigrants started moving away. My dad remembers, "They didn't want to associate with us FOBs."

My mom moved to the US from Hong Kong a few years later with her brother. While she heard that Monterey Park was emerging as a community for Chinese immigrants, she and her brother first settled in Santa Monica because her brother had a friend there whose family could house them for a few months. My mom recalls Santa Monica at the time as predominantly White and pretentious. There were a handful of Hong Kongers in Santa Monica, mostly wealthy international students who attended USC or UCLA. "They didn't want to associate with us uneducated FOBs," my mom recollects. My uncle aspired to go to college and join this elite group of educated internationals, but the family did not have the resources to get him there or to stay in Santa Monica at the time. So my mom and her brother considered their options, and decided to relocate somewhere more economically feasible (and less snobby) to start a family business. At first, they considered resettling in Chinatown, but they heard Chinatown was for "poor immigrants," and Monterey Park was for "better Asians." They decided on Monterey Park because "we didn't want to associate with the lower-class FOBs." They relocated to the ethnoburb, bringing along their dad and sister, and started a family business importing food products from Hong Kong to the growing number of Chinese grocery stores in San Gabriel Valley. My

paternal great-grandfather left his family in South China behind to seek out economic opportunity, becoming the neighborhood lap cheong dealer and filling a niche in San Francisco
Chinatown's ethnic economy, and here came my mom, his
granddaughter-in-law, almost fifty years later, filling a similar
niche in Monterey Park's ethnoburb economy.

Reflecting on this time in their lives, my parents consistently and ominously reference avoiding or being avoided by
some other group of Asians. While the ethnoburb served as
a landing pad for my parents as new immigrants, it was also
the site of intra-ethnic and intra-racial conflict. With any influx of a new group, the preexisting community is forced to
reckon with who they are, and who they aren't. They negotiate
and construct ethnic and racial definitions around status and
perceived foreignness. Some Asian Americans may disassociate from poorer, less assimilated immigrants as an attempt
to protect themselves and bring them adjacency to Whiteness.

Growing up in the ethnoburb, I similarly felt the need to
make distinctions to differentiate myself from "those Asians
moving in," even when I, in fact, am a product of "those
Asians." About a decade prior to the incident in the library, I
was around ten, and my cousin and I were in the back seat of
my dad's car. We were driving to a Hong Kong cafe at an Asian
strip mall somewhere in our neighborhood. My cousin was
visiting from Cupertino, a Northern California counterpart
to San Gabriel Valley, with high proportions of white-collar
Asian immigrants. During the car ride, my cousin excitedly
shared how her city was getting newsworthy attention.

"We were in the local paper! Because there are so many
Asians in Cupertino, it's causing White people to leave! They

called it ASIAN INVASION and WHITE FLIGHT!!!" She waved her hands in the air.

"Oh my God, there are *so* many Asians!" I matched her fervor, not really knowing what we were yelling about.

Driving past 99 Ranch, we unironically spoke of the influx of Asian immigrants as some kind of intrusion, and the exodus of White families as an unfortunate, inevitable side effect. We were in an unspoken agreement that we were obviously exempt and distinguished from "those Asians moving in," as we were meanwhile gluttonously gorging on wontons, egg noodles, congee, and rice rolls cooked by "those Asians moving in." I disassociated from my community as I looked at our ethnoburb through the White gaze. The nativist, anti-immigrant through line of White supremacy trespassed the protective boundaries of the ethnoburb and into my ten-year-old consciousness. I gasped and clutched my metaphorical pearls over the scandal of Asian invasion and White flight, as I slurped another spoonful of preserved egg–and-pork congee.

Sociologists Jennifer Lee and Min Zhou theorize that because Asian connotes foreigner status, which is often stigmatized, it constrains identity options for the children of Asian immigrants. Asians born in the US may feel the need to assert native-born status because America frequently identifies all Asians as foreigners, which threatens our sense of belonging as Americans. Lee and Zhou define this as the second generation's "immigrant shadow,"[8] or the need to make clear distinctions between themselves and "FOBs" in order to protect their native-born status. I have no doubt these claims were true when these studies were conducted and still feel true for many today. My husband, who emigrated from the Philippines when he was five, recalls experiencing the most targeted, racialized bullying from other Filipino Americans—in his *own* community—for being an immigrant.

As the more established group is confronted with growing numbers of new immigrants and their perceived differences, particularly around foreignness, education, and status, they often respond by asserting symbolic boundaries. Santa Monica elite Hong Kongers distinguished themselves from "lower-class" Cantonese immigrants in Chinatown and Monterey Park, even if they all spoke the same dialect, ate the same food, and shared the same homeland. Within weeks in the US, my mom made sure to disassociate from Chinatown. The longtime Monterey Park residents, both White and people of color, held a growing fear that their neighborhoods were turning into ethnic enclaves and Chinatowns. Upon returning to Monterey Park, a third-generation Japanese American resident complained, "Damn it, where the hell did all these Chinese come from? Shit, this isn't our town anymore."[9] Ethnoburbs are sites to negotiate racial identity and boundaries, with definitions of insider and outsider expanding and contracting in response to demographic changes. In non-White spaces like SGV, White racial logics infiltrate and shape how we exclude, other, and belong to one another.

WEI LI, A CHINESE AMERICAN GEOGRAPHER, FIRST PROPOSED the term "ethnoburb" to describe the hybridity of ethnic enclaves and middle-class suburbs: suburban ethnic clusters of people and businesses.[10] Fueled by foreign capital, ethnoburb immigrants redefined the entire landscape of the suburb, and instigated an economic boom. The growth of Chinese American banking institutions, along with the political and economic factors that prompted the migration of wealthy ethnic Chinese from Taiwan and Hong Kong, played an important role in facilitating the Chinese economic growth in Monterey Park. With their resources, Chinese immigrants bought homes and started businesses with distinct Chinese- and Vietnamese-language signs to cater to co-ethnics and fellow Asian transplants. Valley Boulevard, which runs through ten cities in San Gabriel Valley, became home to Asian-owned malls, commercial plazas, office complexes, shops, hotels, and industrial plants, often with trilingual signage in Chinese, Vietnamese, and English. Asian immigrants transformed neglected strip malls into prosperous Asian marketplaces and forged a sense of permanence and community. Monterey Park, and eventually the rest of San Gabriel valley, began to be referred to as "Little Taipei" or the "Chinese Beverly Hills" by journalists and Chinese diasporic media.[11] By the 1980s, Monterey Park was known as "the first suburban Chinatown," converting San Gabriel Valley from predominantly White suburbs into an Asian-majority ecosystem with a conspicuous and diverse first-generation, unassimilated immigrant presence.

The ethnoburb troubles the American construction of the suburbs as static sites of Whiteness and socioeconomic mobility. The majority of new immigrants, especially those with resources, bypassed urban ethnic enclaves like Chinatown that previously served as immigrant gateway cities and settled immediately into suburbs instead. Further, Zhou argues that this direct insertion of new Asian immigrants into traditionally White middle-class suburbs offends the conventional understanding of immigration and assimilation. Ethnoburb immigrants were non-White, didn't always speak English, made considerably less effort to acculturate into Whiteness, and many of them were already educated and affluent. They broke the bounds of the American imagination of an immigrant. In addition to higher levels of education and incomes, many ethnoburb immigrants also possessed expansive and transnational social networks that shaped their reluctance to acculturate. They did not need to learn English or go through the ethnic enclave in order to reach a middle-class dream of financial stability. The ethnoburb was not a "staging ground"[12] for somewhere better or Whiter. The ethnoburb was the final desired destination.

I, on the other hand, longed to get out of the ethnoburb. With an enduring interest in social issues and activism, the ethnoburb felt too insular, apolitical, and homogeneous to me. How could I possibly make a difference in this manicured suburb with SAT prep schools and upwardly mobile, civically unengaged Asians all around me? I was naive and presumptuous, and thought I was better than the ethnoburb. Now, having moved away from San Gabriel Valley for over ten years to self-actualize in more "interesting" spaces, I find myself longing to go back. Paying exorbitant rent to live somewhere trendy is overrated and unsustainable. I want Asian strip malls, I want Hong Kong cafes, and I want my child to grow up hearing Cantonese regularly and know that we're not yelling, that's just our default volume.

In actuality, the ethnoburb was not apolitical or insular

at all. It was and remains a site of resistance against the confining, White imagination of suburbia. With the emergence of Monterey Park as an Asian ethnoburb, questions over group identity, spatial boundaries, and the character of Monterey Park became politicized. Nativist White residents were at the forefront of erecting boundaries of belonging that stigmatized first-generation immigrants. In addition to Asian businesses changing the aesthetic and cultural identity of Monterey Park, Asian immigrants took on local politics. This direct insertion of unassimilated Asian immigrants into traditionally White suburbs and its institutions troubled conventional American understandings of who an immigrant is, the norms they should follow, and how they should behave.

On November 8, 1983, Lily Lee Chen, a first-generation immigrant from Taiwan, was inaugurated in Monterey Park as the first Chinese American mayor in the nation. Chen was relatable, charismatic, and not assimilated. The *Los Angeles Times* described Chen's speech as "accented with pauses and grammatical errors, characteristic of someone speaking in their second language."[13] In their 1985 article, Chen shared that she enjoyed dressing in bright reds and jade greens, despite being told by her consultant to look more subdued because her bright colors made her appear "aggressive." During her campaign, she was met with fierce resistance from White residents, who commonly took down her neighborhood campaign signs. As a response, Chen worked tirelessly on voter engagement among Asian Americans and Latinos, publishing multilingual voter handbooks, registering voters, and building relationships with ethnic communities, including working with Cesar Chavez to support the Latinos in Southern

California. The same year as Chen's election, Monterey Park's five-member city council became multiethnic, with two Mexican Americans, one Filipino American, one Chinese American, and one White council member.

As Monterey Park became touted as a "successful suburban melting pot" by journalists and even won an "All-American City" award in 1985 for its civic engagement and racial diversity, White flight accelerated and resentment festered among the minority of White residents. The large influx and increasing influence of Chinese immigrants over a short period of time caused racial tension to build, with mounting struggles over cultural differences, language barriers, and explicit mistrust of immigrants. Chinese businesses, political candidates, religious institutions, and entrepreneurs became racialized targets of nativist animus. A particularly contentious conflict emerged over the proliferation of business signs in languages other than English. In 1986, White hostility among the remaining White residents swept the council members of color out of office, and replaced them with three long-established White residents, who promptly launched an anti-immigrant, "English-only" campaign attacking the proliferation of business signage in Chinese.

The "English-only" movement in Monterey Park reflects the struggle to control the identity and narrative of a built environment. It represents the tension between America's idea of how immigrants should assimilate, and how ethnoburb immigrants instead created their own unassimilable institutions and communities. Frank Arcuri, one of the Monterey Park residents and community activists who started the "English-only" petition campaign, insisted, "Immigrants are welcome here, but they must realize that English is the language we use in America. . . . They must realize they are making a negative impact on our city. They must adapt to our ways. They must use our language and respect our culture." On his ballot statement for council member, he wrote, "We must do something about Monterey Park's haphazard, uncontrolled growth. . . . We must require the use of English on all business and advertising signs. . . . I believe that our American heritage comes before any ethnic loyalty. We must join together to plan our city's future, not as members of different 'multiethnic communities,' but as Americans."[14]

The nativist, inflammatory rhetoric Arcuri employed to speak about immigrants is as American as apple pie, comparable to replacement theory touted by White nationalist conspiracists today. In response, Mayor Chen proposed an ordinance requiring some English on all foreign-language signs, with an English street address as a minimum requirement. The ordinance, which eventually passed, was unsatisfactory to both Asian and White residents. Asian newcomers criticized the ordinance to be unconstitutional, and White residents complained that their demands were watered down. The English-only conflict illustrates the deeper, ideological tensions behind an increasingly diverse and polyglot constituency, composed of politically active immigrants, and nostalgic White residents desperately (and at times violently) clinging on to institutional power and a homogeneous past. Mayor Chen had to not only account for the maze of conflicts between recent immigrants and older White residents but contend with the fundamental character, unassimilability, and future of Monterey Park.

TRADITIONALLY, SOCIOLOGISTS OF IMMIGRATION AND ASSIMI-
lation theorists believed that all immigrant groups would eventually assimilate and integrate into White Protestant American
institutions, culture, and society. They argued that doing so
would be in the best interests of immigrants. They were also
all White scholars. For the most part, what they theorized was
true for European immigrants. However, Asian immigrants
in the ethnoburb remained proudly unassimilable and transnational. While the ethnoburb was their final destination, they
maintained diasporic ties. Many with socioeconomic privilege
shuttled back and forth to their home countries. In her theory
of "segmented assimilation," Zhou argues that the deliberate
preservation of ethnic values, ties, and institutions is what
actually acclimates non-White immigrants to the US, pointing
to the case of transnational Chinese immigrants in the ethnoburb. It is our diasporic connections to our motherlands and
our ethnic communities, not necessarily our assimilation into
Whiteness, that help us thrive in the US.

My uncle started a family in the US, but continued his
business in Hong Kong and China. My cousins grew up bicul-
tural, with dual passports and roots that spanned across the
Pacific Ocean. My parents, who had no intention of moving
back to Hong Kong, still maintained strong and close linkages
with their family and friends back home. They prioritized taking me back to Hong Kong whenever possible, which helped
cultivate my sense of self and home outside of the US. I may
have felt embarrassed of my popo, at times insecure about
my "immigrant shadow," but I always knew I belonged to my
grandparents and extended family in Hong Kong.

We were privileged to take the red-eye from LAX to Hong

Kong every few years, spending Christmas through New Year's with my yeye, mama, aunties, uncles, and cousins, and my parents' childhood friends, their chosen family. Once we landed, the three of us would often split up. Nice knowing you, parents, but I've got people to see and places to be. My parents would catch up with their friends, while I would gallivant around Hong Kong with my yeye, mama, and cousins. As an only child, I loved this arrangement and getting to spend time with my village. We rode every form of public transit—bus, train, gondola, ferry, pedicab—because my grandma thought it would be fun for us. My grandparents stuffed my cousins and me with bo lo bao and egg waffles and spicy fish balls off the street, brought us to dim sum with their friends, and gave us lectures on how "Louies are the best" and "America is a mess" and "you better know where you come from." I loved it all. There was a specificity and celebration of who we were that I rarely experienced in the US.

When it was time to leave, we always took the cheapest New Year's Day flight, and a wordless melancholy would fall over my parents and me. Our family would suddenly feel small and lonely. We would spend the first day of the new year quietly longing for what we'd just left, never naming this diasporic grief to one another. These trips reflected our transient, transnational form of family making. Our ongoing ties to our homeland, culture, and people, not our assimilation into Whiteness, was what helped me feel rooted and flourish, even if it came with this diasporic ache on New Year's Day. Returning to Hong Kong defined my coming of age and self-actualization, not in individualistic terms, but as somebody in the diaspora inextricably linked to a larger village.

As I grew, I eventually replaced my disavowal of San Gabriel Valley with affection and appreciation. I treasure the audacious, unassimilable pieces of the ethnoburb, as I am also challenged by the economic exploitation of poor and undocumented workers that made my life in the ethnoburb possible. I labor to exorcise the through line of Whiteness that infiltrated our space and my own consciousness, pitting us against Black and Latino communities and cultivating conditions for abuse, inequality, and anti-Blackness. I embrace my ethnoburb, in all of its limitations, possibilities, and unassimilability.

Ultimately, I don't belong in or to the US, nor do I aspire to. I construct my own belonging like the ethnoburb: by finding my people, building our own ecosystem, and maintaining ties across borders. I am not "torn between two cultures," as they say, because I occupy a third space in the diaspora, from where a collective identity emerges that is neither repulsed by foreignness nor longing for Whiteness, but adamantly unassimilable.

diasporic ache

2

PWI-WAA (Predominantly White Institutions with "A Lot" of Asians)

I once heard the University of California, Irvine (UCI) referred to as the University of Chinese Immigrants. Ethnoburbs felt like pipelines to the UC and Cal State system, and UCI is home to large numbers of second generation Asian Americans from San Gabriel Valley and surrounding Southern California ethnoburbs. By the time I was in college in the early 2010s, UCI was 43 percent Asian. Even though UCI is a highly competitive and well-resourced university, I refused to go there. Today, the school has become so selective that I'm sure I would not even get admitted. UCI at the time felt too much like an extension of San Gabriel Valley to me, and I arrogantly thought of myself as above it. I wanted to live somewhere "more interesting," with a smaller strip-mall-per-square-mile ratio. SGV, and by extension heavily Asian spaces like UCI, felt too limited and insular for my ambitions. I turned down my scholarship to UCI and, to my parents' dismay, illogically moved farther away to Oakland to enroll in Mills College instead, a lower-ranked school, just to get away from SGV. The tools and resources of the ethnoburb, including shadow education and good schools, afforded me the option, urgency, and entitlement to choose out of it altogether.

My family and I were aware that Asian Americans were visibly growing as a demographic in higher education, but it was not guaranteed that I would necessarily be one of them. My parents always seemed to feel behind, anxiously comparing me to richer, smarter children of their college-educated Hart-Celler peers. They placed colossal stakes around my education to overcompensate for not having graduated from college themselves. As early as preschool, my mom drove over thirty minutes each way, out of the ethnoburb and into a Whiter neighborhood, for me to spend my mornings at a Montessori school, learning how to count, spell, and read in English. My parents had no idea what Montessori was, but they heard through the ethnoburb grapevine that this particular school had attentive teachers and a fair amount of Chinese families.

My childhood is a series of costly sacrifices my parents made for my education. After Montessori, we relocated from South San Gabriel, a more affordable and heavily immigrant part of SGV, to rent in San Marino, the highly manicured and probably Whitest part of SGV at the time, in order to attend the schools. As a five-year-old, I loved this move. Our new neighborhood had sidewalks, tree-lined streets, and flowers. We had a backyard that housed blue jays, squirrels, and the occasional family of skunks. I sang to my creatures every morning. We lived across the street from another Cantonese family that had children my age.

Like other Asian immigrant families in SGV, neighborhood and school choice represented much more than where we would live and which schools I would attend. For my parents, these factors determined the peers I would be around (White and East Asian were always the desired peer groups), access to more options throughout my life, and the possibility of eventual class mobility. Moving to San Marino represented proximity to Whiteness without completely leaving the safety and comforts of the ethnoburb. 99 Ranch was still a fifteen-minute drive away, and so was the predominantly White private school in Pasadena I would attend in a few years.

Jennifer Lee and Min Zhou describe much of my family's experiences with and attitudes about education in *The Asian American Achievement Paradox*. Even though my parents were not necessarily part of the hyperselective wave of professional Chinese immigrants post-1965, we were privileged because of strategies and resources in the ethnoburb. San Gabriel Valley had a strong public elementary school, as well as supplementary education in the form of standardized test preparation created by middle class co-ethnics. Being part of an ethnic community gave us access to intangible resources as well, including the dissemination of relevant intel about education, such as information about school rankings, SAT classes, and college admissions processes. Lee and Zhou argue that these supplemental ethnic resources and collective strategies mitigate class disadvantages and provide immigrant families with a road map to mobility.

It was through the ethnoburb Asian mom network that my parents learned about Montessori, San Marino elementary schools, and eventually Westridge. At the time, Westridge was a mostly White, college preparatory school for girls. Its campus, which resembled a prestigious university more than a primary school, was tucked away in the old-ass-White-money part of Pasadena, past San Marino and definitively out of the ethnoburb. Westridge embodied a White elitism that my parents and I had never encountered before. On our family campus visit, articulate fourth graders in their starched, pleated white uniforms explained private school traditions to us, like class rings, big and little sisters, songs in Latin, and the infamous Greek and Roman "houses." Very foreign, very Hogwarts.

As we toured the extravagant, meticulously polished campus and learned about small class sizes, pedagogical rigor, and college admission successes, my parents fell head over heels in love. They recognized Westridge as a particular gateway institution that would change the trajectory of our lives, opening up opportunities not only for my education but for my eventual career, status, and our belonging in this country. Westridge was the portal not just to stability but to prestige. As a third grader, I felt the weight of this campus visit as my parents talked incessantly about it, placing massive stakes around my application.

When Westridge cleared me through the first round of admissions and invited me to interview and attend another campus visit on my own, my mom gave me a pep talk: "We're going to *make* them remember your name." She instructed me to shake hands, introduce myself, and remember the names of every single person I met on campus that day. This included everyone from the dean of admissions, the lower school director, school administrators, teachers' classrooms I visited, fourth-grade student "hosts," and parent volunteers who walked me from one meeting to the next. It was a lot of names, and I did not learn any of them.

I was an artistic child and enjoyed drawing at the time. After the visit, my mom instructed me to draw portraits inspired by my day at Westridge. She then went to Kinko's to copy my artwork into greeting cards, which we used to write personalized thank-you notes to everybody I met that day. This was the beginning of monetizing my hobbies for ambition over leisure, which I will probably never unlearn. I ended each card with "P.S. This is a little something I drew, inspired by my day at Westridge!" as a strategically placed humble brag. I repeated my mom's mantra to myself—*We're going to make these fuckers remember my name*—as I wrote, "Thank you for the day at Westridge!" in purple marker in my best handwriting. We were calculated and crafty and a little unhinged. Whatever it took.

Going through Westridge's admission process instilled a neuroticism and deficit mentality in me, as I realized school choice was not necessarily about learning, but about class, status, and money. My friend Elizabeth also applied to Westridge the same year. Going through the process together, it seemed like Elizabeth would have a smoother time than I would. Not only did teachers love her (she was a precocious kid with an undeniable charm), it felt like Elizabeth's family, who were also immigrants but came to the US at a much earlier age and went to college in the country, somehow knew the ins and outs of the application process. It helped that this would be their family's second child in private school. While we were ridden with anxiety, they seemed comfortable and self-assured. My parents and I navigated the American educational system for the first time together, and now we had to decode this elusive private school Latin-singing witchcraft together. Further, my parents worried constantly about how we would afford tuition if I actually got accepted. Applying to Westridge taught me what it meant to feel behind, a sentiment my parents drilled into me, and a feeling that is continually familiar (even if untrue) today.

My parents moved zip codes, deferred their own dreams of starting their own business, and suffered through abusive work environments for a stable paycheck to afford rent in the right school district, Westridge tuition, and whatever other expenses it took to support my education. My dad developed chronic migraines and eventually debilitating anxiety and depression due to forbearing exploitive employers and a grueling commute of one hundred and forty miles each day in Los Angeles traffic, selling used cars to cover the costs of my education. They communicated that this was simply part of the critical decisions necessary to insert me into the most prestigious spaces we dared to access. All three of us would do whatever it took for me, and by extension us, to advance. This communal orientation and determination tied my own achievement to my family. It was never just about me, the individual. It was always about the three of us as a collective.

I don't share all of this to beat my drum to the problematic "battle hymn of the tiger mom." In actuality, my parents matched their high expectations and sacrifices with abundant support. It wasn't ever me against them, nagging and coercing me into the perfect A+ Asian. It was always us three

against the pressures and disadvantages of being first generation, us three against the American education system we were
determined to hack. They never got angry at me for bringing
home Bs, Cs, and even Ds (I was very much a mediocre, and
sometimes failing, student for many years regardless of my
effort). Instead, they asked me what I needed to succeed, and
worked with me to find more support. They gave me freedom
to choose my own classes and major and career path, always
emphasizing that passion and heart beget excellence. They
were and are still my biggest supporters, even if they don't
always understand what I'm doing.

Supportive systems in the ethnoburb, built by and for
immigrants and their children, enabled me to access White
spaces like Westridge and reject where I came from. These
educational opportunities shaped my racial consciousness.
While my urgency to leave the ethnoburb can be attributed
to normal teenage restlessness to get out of my hometown, it
was also shaped by my own internalized racism, cultivated by
nine years of exposure and assimilation into White elitism at
Westridge. I internalized the individualistic need to become
someone significant, and assumed that this could not happen
in or near an ethnoburb, among my own community.

As I applied to colleges, I was not consciously trying to get
closer to Whiteness, but I was adamant to free myself of the
distinct Chinese-ness and immigrant shadow of the ethnoburb and majority Asian spaces. I avoided schools like UCI
where Asians are "overrepresented"; schools that I now coin
PWI-WAAs: Predominantly White Institutions with "A Lot" of
Asians. As I insensitively joked about the University of Chinese Immigrants being full of "FOBs," I never interrogated

our actual numbers, our agency, or the ongoing dominance of Whiteness and legacy admissions at these schools. I had no idea what our so-called representation actually implied. I judged our collective visibility, heightened by unassimilated Asian international students, as something to disassociate from. As I rolled my eyes over the "Asian invasion" of the UC system, I was naive of the fact that just thirty years prior, Asian Americans were among the most underrepresented minority groups in UC schools, facing barriers to higher education that required affirmative action to overcome.[1]

US educational institutions were exclusive White spaces that Asian Americans could not access until the 1960s, and did not have any visible presence in until the 1980s. During and after the civil rights movement, discrimination in education became the target of breakthrough civil rights cases and efforts, including Brown v. Board of Education in 1954, which declared "separate but equal" unconstitutional, and University of California v. Bakke in 1978, which established the constitutionality of affirmative action. As a result of these measures, the US Office for Civil Rights required institutions of higher education to develop affirmative action programs specifically geared toward hiring qualified minorities, which included "Negroes, Spanish-surnamed persons, American Indians, and Orientals."[2] Asian Americans, at the time labeled "Orientals," were designated beneficiaries of affirmative action and eventually gained admission to predominantly White institutions. Affirmative action created opportunities for communities of color, and aspired to destabilize the dominance and maintenance of Whiteness in higher education.[3]

By the mid-1980s, Asian American representation in colleges and universities increased as an outcome of affirmative action, selective immigration policies that favored professional and educated immigrants, and the development of ethnoburb educational resources that supported children of immigrants to pursue higher education. In 1976, the number of Asian American students across all levels of higher education was 198,000. In 1988, that figure increased to 497,000, growing from 2 to 4 percent of the total number of students.[4] The percentage growth of Asian Americans in higher education actually exceeded that of Black students in this time frame. In 1970, 7.8 percent of college students were Black. In 1980, that number increased by 1.3 percentage points to 9.1 percent.[5]

In California between the 1970s and 1980s, the Asian American population at UC Berkeley jumped dramatically from 5.2 percent to 20 percent of total enrolled students, while Black students grew from 4 to 5 percent and Latino students from 2 to 6 percent.[6] In this same time period, the Asian American proportion of California's total population only increased from 3 to 5 percent, while the Black proportion grew from 7 to 8 percent and the Latino proportion increased from 13 to 19 percent.[7] Because our growth in the UC system was not proportional to our overall population growth in the state of California, we became "overrepresented" in higher education according to statistical parity measures.

Public perception of Asian Americans changed in response to these demographic shifts. The New York Times published an article in 1981 titled, "Rapid Rise in Students of Asian Origin Causing Problems at Berkeley Campus," referencing the large numbers of Asian immigrants and children of immigrants who supposedly struggled with English language proficiency, yet excelled in mathematics. These Asian students occupied large proportions of incoming classes, and "disturbed" other groups.[8] By 1984, Berkeley administrators no longer considered Asian Americans eligible for affirmative action outreach and support. Administrators and policymakers aimed for "general parity between racial and ethnic composition of undergraduate enrollment and that of the state population in general,"[9] and limited admissions slots put Asian American minority status on slippery ground. Proportionality became the measure of racial progress, decisively overturning the perception of Asian Americans as discriminated minorities in need of affirmative action. According to statistical parity measures, we were over-represented in higher education compared to our overall share of the US population, thus "overcoming" discrimination and "outgrowing" the need for affirmative action protections.[10]

Today, it is no secret that Asian and Asian American students have a visible presence on colleges and universities, traditionally created to exclusively educate White males. Instead of recognizing the political and structural factors behind the growth of Asian Americans in higher education, policymakers and media conjured culturally essentialist arguments that associated Asians with achievement, reifying the model minority stereotype as the reason for this growth. This ideological representation, along with the highly visible demographic change in higher education, sets the backdrop for the public discourse and racial politics of achievement and representation today.

Affirmative action is highly contested, and with Asian Americans at the center of its debates, the issue is possibly one of the most divisive among us. While mainstream media often reduces us to objects, rather than subjects, of these debates, scholars OiYan Poon, Megan Segoshi, and Jennifer Lee, among others, assert that it is a mistake, however, to assume that Asian Americans are passive agents of this issue. In actuality, Asian American civic organizations have long histories of defending affirmative action alongside Black and Latino community organizations.[11] Despite public discourse and perceptions that Asian Americans oppose affirmative action, AAPI Data found in 2022 that 69 percent of Asian Americans favored affirmative action.[12] While there is variation among Asian ethnic groups, the study found that all Asian groups surveyed were more likely to support than oppose affirmative action. Only one group stands apart in opposition: Chinese Americans. And because Chinese is synecdoche for all Asians, their attitudes are mistaken to represent the political views of all Asian Americans.[13]

As some of the most vocal Chinese Americans align with White conservatives on this issue, they buy into the narrative that they are the exceptional, deserving minority, and that affirmative action robs them of opportunities to make room for supposedly less-deserving Black and Latino populations. But even while Chinese Americans are least likely to support affirmative action, nearly three-fifths (59 percent) favor the policy, and Chinese American support has increased since 2020.[14] Why these particular Chinese Americans are unique (and so forthright) in their opposition of affirmative action is a question that continues to keep me up at night. Perhaps it is because Chinese Americans are one of the oldest groups in the US, giving us time over generations to assimilate and internalize White racial logics about merit and achievement. Many of us may subscribe to these ideologies because they appear to validate our struggles in this country. Perhaps these narratives comfort us and make us feel seen in our efforts to belong here. The zero-sum conditions of affirmative action rhetoric may trigger memories of scarcity in us, activating a defensive reaction to fiercely protect what we believe we deserve. Whatever the reasons that lie beneath, our racial positionings and longings are entangled with the racial politics of achievement, and many in our communities paradoxically commit to dismantle the very affirmative action policies that facilitated access for us in the first place.

The model minority myth became foundational to the American imagination as of the 1980s, marking a decisive shift in public perception of Asian Americans from affirmative action beneficiaries to "model victims."[15] Fundamentally, the model minority stereotype upholds a mythical racial politic of individualism and meritocracy, while justifying racial discrimination against Black Americans. To explain poverty among Black Americans, the controversial Moynihan report, published in 1965 by Assistant Secretary of Labor Daniel Patrick Moynihan, promulgated the poverty thesis, which pointed to an autonomous, self-perpetuating culture of poverty among Black Americans that transmitted across generations. At the same time, the report constructed Asian Americans as the model minority to counter Black Americans and their perceived lack of work ethic.

By emphasizing individual, familial, and cultural differences and "deficiencies," the media and policymakers propagated harmful stereotypes like the "welfare queen," while diverting attention away from the gross structural and historical inequalities that produced racial inequality in the first place. These neoconservative policy paradigms relied on evoking "culture" to explain both poor and exceptional outcomes, especially in education. They juxtaposed Asian Americans to Black Americans as the model minority with cultural and familial "achievement orientation."[16] This racialization of Asian Americans as the model minority conveniently operated to discipline other racialized groups, engender victim-blaming explanations for inequality, delegitimize racial justice organizing, and distract attention away from systems of White dominance.

To this day, we are upheld by Whiteness because our bodies in PWIs justify the fiction that racial barriers in these institutions (and in this country) no longer exist. Our achievement is manipulated to argue that race-based policies like affirmative action are outdated, because if Asian Americans are able to overcome racism and go to Harvard, there are no excuses for everybody else. At the same time, we are paradoxically perceived as "taking over" American higher education, because our presence threatens the Whiteness that these institutions traditionally serve. This disturbing contradiction leaves us in a place of racial precarity, simultaneously othered and praised by PWIs and higher education.

Scholars suggest that Asian Americans are the "middleman minority"[17] in the Black/White binary, constituting a "racial bourgeoisie"[18] as the intermediate group on America's bipolar racial scale, which places Whites at the top, Black Americans at the bottom, and other groups somewhere in between.[19] Claire Jean Kim's seminal theory on racial triangulation moves analysis beyond a Black/White hierarchy, as she argues that Asian Americans are "racially triangulated" vis-à-vis White and Black

Americans through two types of simultaneous, connected processes: 1) relative valorization, whereby Whites valorize Asians as the model minority relative to Black Americans in order to dominate both groups, and 2) civic ostracism, whereby Whites construct Asian Americans as the yellow peril, unassimilable and perpetually foreign, in order to exclude us from the body politic.[20] Racial triangulation explains the racial structure that maintains White dominance by holding Asian Americans in a contradictory, unsettled position and pitting minoritized groups against one another.

In all of this theorizing, scholars assert what we intuitively know: Asian Americans are neither Black nor White. But how have the invasive model minority myth and its implications on racial politics and education affected our individual and collective racial consciousness? How do we internalize these narratives, and how do they shape how we see ourselves and other racial groups? These questions reflect the larger, unspoken sociopolitical backdrop as my parents and I navigated Westridge, standardized tests, and eventually college applications. Because of the insularity and racial homogeneity of the ethnoburb, the White dominance and anti-Blackness were often implicit. Racial hierarchy persisted through the urgency to move to neighborhoods and schools with more White and affluent East Asian students, and the assumed antipathy toward zip codes and school districts with large Latino and Black populations. Although the ethnoburb was heavily Asian and Latino, the racial politics of achievement were expressed and reproduced through resources like supplementary education that exclusively catered to Asian Americans. In my SAT boot camps, the students were overwhelmingly Asian American.

The racial homogeneity of these resources communicated the myth that we were the ones who needed supplementary education, and we were the ones who deserved to access them.

In Jacqueline Yi and Nathan Todd's study on Asian American college students, they found greater internalized model minority myth, particularly achievement orientation, was directly associated with greater anti-Black attitudes.[21] When Asian Americans believed that their racial group was more academically and economically successful because of their "stronger values" in achievement and hard work compared to other racial minorities, they were more likely to believe that Black Americans did not possess such values and therefore were less successful. In SGV, these attitudes also extended to our Latino peers and neighbors, who my family members regularly stereotyped as lazy and not academically oriented.

Yi and Todd's study also found that greater internalized model minority myth directly predicted greater adherence to color-blind racist ideology. Scholars draw parallels between the model minority myth and color-blind racist ideology, defined by sociologist Eduardo Bonilla-Silva as a type of legitimizing ideology that preserves racial inequality by denying or minimizing the existence of racial differences and institutional racism. Color-blind racist ideology facilitates anti-Black attitudes and opposition to affirmative action, upholding the idea that inequality is a result of individual, rather than systemic, failure.[22] Another study found that color-blindness among Asian Americans corresponded with minimization of one's racial identity and lower perceptions of oneself as a target of racism.[23] If you refuse to see color, you also refuse to see when you've been racially discriminated against.

I grew up on color-blind racist ideology, in an era of un-questioned and tokenizing representation: Black sidekick, mean (and usually silent) Asian girl, White hero. See: *Ten Things I Hate About You, Clueless,* and *Bring It On,* my favorite guilty pleasures, which, looking back, were the worst places to derive my racial ideologies in the 2000s. Westridge at the time was an all-girls preparatory school serving a White feminist agenda: we discussed gender pervasively, but our vocabularies did not include race, class, immigration status, sexuality, or other forms of identity and power. Instead, we were "the colors of the world," with White, Asian, Black, and racially ambiguous Brown children on the covers of our textbooks. Locating myself among the color-blind White feminism of the 2000s at West-ridge became an endeavor full of delusions and contradictions. I tangibly felt my racial and class differences, yet at the same time had no language to name my own experiences. I made several White friends, and we got along well enough for them to invite me to their homes for sleepovers, but I always had to leave by ten o'clock because sleepovers are the immigrant child's forbidden fruit. Despite my attending this school (and these birthday parties) for nine years, White parents neglected to learn my name and perpetually confused me with other Asian girls in our class.

I also had a handful of friends who looked like me. Our incoming fourth-grade class of forty had nine Asian American students. I thought I was supposed to relate to them because the parents thought we were the same person anyway, but our backgrounds were vastly different. It was among my Asian American friends that I actually perceived the most profound divergence, particularly around class and family background.

My Asian American peers came from more assimilated families, speaking English at home with parents who had established careers in the US. Their parents talked about sports and alma maters with the White parents, even taking ski trips to Aspen over the holidays together. They invited us once, and we had to find an excuse to defer because it was socially unacceptable to say, "We can't afford your absurdly expensive trip to Aspen—are you insane?!" I often witnessed my mother shrink around Westridge parents, which is painful to recollect because she's a Cantonese woman, and I use "Cantonese" as a synonym for loud and proud and indomitable. Yet around these private school parents, my mother got lost in their cultural references and confidence and quick conversations, unable to jump through the language and cultural hoops to get into their social circles.

We were trained not to "see" color, class, or difference of any sort, so I struggled to name the ways I felt like an outsider, even though I had friends. Additionally, my daily commute from my immigrant ethnoburb to elite White Pasadena left me in a mental state of racial placelessness. Both places felt like home, but only to distinct parts of me. It was the beginning of code switching, compartmentalizing, and fracturing my whole self to fit into these disparate spaces.

Looking back on this time, the failures of color-blind racist ideology are apparent. This way of interpreting the world prevented me from understanding myself and those around me. Acknowledging race and class differences was taboo, yet these structures were operative everywhere, all the time. Our fourth-grade class only had one Latina student and two Black students out of our class of forty. In my nine years at

Westridge, I remember three Asian American teachers and one Black teacher, Monique (the only teacher we referred to without honorifics), who taught dance. We had one Latino PE teacher, and the other Latino adults we saw on campus worked as custodial staff.

I noticed Black students often spent their lunches in Monique's office, but I never understood why. I thought they were cliquey and exclusive: loudly blasting music videos on Monique's desktop, laughing, dancing, having a good time, usually only with other Black students. I was juvenile, judgmental, and probably jealous of their camaraderie. Only in adulthood have I considered that Monique's office possibly served as a haven for Black students. Westridge could feel like an elitist campus run by rich White girls. Their names were literally written on the plaques, bricks, and walls of buildings throughout campus, honoring their families' donations to the school. Westridge was a place where non-Black teachers and students openly said the n-word, and Black students were disproportionately disciplined for things the rest of us often got away with, like cell phones on campus or dressing out of uniform. I'm sure there were many other anti-Black offenses and instances of violence that I did not have the eyes to see at the time. Despite the institution's reluctance to recognize it, race and class were pervasive: in social cliques, in discipline, in teacher-student-parent interactions, in our commutes to school, in the simultaneous invisibility and hypervisibility of Black students, in "free dress Fridays." Race and class were written on the walls, hidden in plain sight.

Color-blind racist ideology gave me zero tools to understand the racial and socioeconomic dynamics at my PWI. Looking back, I was simultaneously othered, invisibilized, and privileged. My experience at Westridge leads me to contemplate the complicated, implicit race and class dynamics at work among Asian Americans in these spaces. I question the experience Asian Americans have of exclusion and integration in PWIs, as well as our roles in maintaining oppression and anti-Blackness in these spaces. I felt racially placeless in White elite Pasadena, at odds with affluent Asian Americans, and unaware of the normalized, unchecked anti-Blackness on our campus. What does it mean for us to rely on and perpetuate color-blind racist ideology, even when it fails us and those around us? In the ideological divide and dismantling of affirmative action, these are the questions that come to a head.

Linda, one of my Asian American peers from Westridge, identifies as socially progressive. After Westridge, Linda went to an Ivy League (nobody was surprised), where she met her husband. The two of them have all the right language to talk about everything smart, from travel to art to investments to politics to Michelin-rated restaurants. Since becoming a mother to three daughters, Linda started leaning more politically conservative, particularly around affirmative action. She tells me she wants her girls to have the best opportunities and futures possible, and she believes affirmative action takes possibilities away from them because they are Asian and affluent. I remind her, "They are also double legacy."

Many of us earnestly want the best for our future generations. We may have internalized the myth that education is determined by scarcity, competition, and zero-sum conditions.

Another's success comes at the expense of ours, and we believe we must clobber and fight to protect the system we've hacked, lest the rules of the game change again to disadvantage us. While this may or may not reflect individuals like Linda, organized Asian American groups against affirmative action rely heavily on the model minority stereotype. They blame "undeserving" Black, Latino, and Native American students who are given "preferential treatment" over high-achieving Asian Americans, yet I never hear them indict the disproportionate admission of underachieving White legacy students. They also perpetuate color-blind racist logics, accusing the act of recognizing racial categories in admissions as racist, while paradoxically highlighting their racial minority status and claiming culturally superior attributes that reify the model minority myth.[24]

White conservative activist Edward Blum and his organization Students for Fair Consideration galvanized and recruited Asian American plaintiffs in lawsuits targeting Harvard, University of North Carolina at Chapel Hill, and the University of Wisconsin at Madison. These lawsuits accused universities of setting quotas and discriminating against Whites and Asian Americans by holding them to higher standards and giving preference to Black, Latino, and Native American applicants. *Students for Fair Admissions v. Harvard* went on to become the landmark Supreme Court case that ultimately dismantled affirmative action. White neoconservative stakeholders succeeded in preying upon Asian American families' (mostly Chinese Americans') real experiences of exclusion and scarcity in education to garner fervent support against affirmative action. Highly organized groups like Asian American Legal

Foundation and Asian American Coalition for Education also submitted legal briefs arguing that high-performing Asian American students were racially discriminated against and passed over because they were Asian, simultaneously pushing for color-blind admissions *and* citing racial discrimination.

Meanwhile, community organizations like Asian American Center for Advancing Justice, Filipino Advocates for Justice, Chinese for Affirmative Action, and Asian American Legal Defense and Education, with long histories of fighting for affirmative action in interracial coalitions, argued that race-based policies like affirmative action are necessary because racism continues to unfairly limit educational opportunities for students of color, including Asian Americans. Throughout the 1980s to today, Asian Americans are rarely acknowledged as direct beneficiaries of affirmative action, even though we continue to benefit from affirmative action programs that increase campus diversity.[25] These advocacy groups commonly cite barriers to higher education among Southeast Asian and Pacific Islander students, who hold college degrees at rates far lower than East and South Asian American counterparts and lower than the national average, and especially benefit from affirmative action.

The discordant ideological divide over affirmative action exposes the fractures in Asian American political identity, bringing the label's utility to unite us into question. On all sides, the struggle reflects our collective attempt to make meaning from the scarcity perpetuated by White systems. Despite the narrative work of progressive Asian American groups, the mainstream conversations on this issue are dominated by the minority of conservative Chinese Americans. Further, in the dialogues and decisions on scholarships, admission, and retention, East Asians, Southeast Asians, and Pacific Islanders are aggregated together, despite census data revealing significant differences across these groups in educational attainment, income levels, English-language proficiency, occupations, and poverty levels.

Pacific Islanders and Asian Americans are amalgamated together, even though there is rarely meaningful inclusion of Pacific Islanders in policy or practice. Pacific Islander Studies scholars like J. Kēhaulani Kauanu and Maenette K. P. Ah Nee-Benham and community advocates requested to not subsume the distinct voices and experiences of Native Hawaiian and Pacific Islanders (NHPI) into an "Asian/Pacific Islander" pan-ethnicity, arguing that the "homogenisation and racialisation [of Pacific Islanders with Asian Americans is] detrimental to [Indigenous] self-determination—a central issue among Pacific Islanders."[26] By conflating nearly fifty ethnic groups together, AAPI as a census category is a perilous and uncertain label that dismisses and maintains inequalities faced by Southeast Asians and Pacific Islanders, while detracting from sovereignty movements distinct to Native Hawaiians and Pacific Islanders. The aggregation of these groups, along with the pervasive model minority stereotype, preserve the perception that all AAPIs are successful, distorting the ways affirmative action serves the interests of many AAPI subgroups that face educational and economic barriers.[27]

Leanne, an undergraduate at Rice University, a highly prestigious PWI-WAA, identifies herself as a first-generation low-income (FGLI) Vietnamese American. Her parents are refugees who relocated to Houston after the US intervention in Vietnam. Since starting at Rice, she struggled to acclimate into life as a college student, support herself financially, and stay afloat academically in a highly competitive and rigorous environment that she believes her high school did not prepare her for. In the process, she found purpose and community in student leadership, organizing around racial justice issues and support for FGLI students on campus. Her days are filled with class, work, service, and committee meetings. In all of these spaces, she reflects, "Rice sees me as White-adjacent." While Asian and Asian American students make up 9 percent of the university's undergraduate student body, Leanne reports that Asian Americans feel invisible in decisions and discussions about racism on campus. Her experience as first-generation, low-income, and Southeast Asian is further invisibilized. Additionally, Asian American students at her institution are by default ineligible for supportive services, scholarships, and opportunities for FGLI students and students of color, leaving her at a loss as she navigates various aspects of university life.

With our alleged overrepresentation in higher education, and PWIs becoming PWI-WAAs, states like Washington and Michigan started counting Asian American students as White. North Thurston Public Schools, in the Olympia area of Washington, for example, went viral for grouping Asian American students with White students, distinct from students of color, in their 2020 student growth report monitoring test scores and graduation rates.[28] The district has since apologized, but they cited Asian American students' overall academic success as the reason to delineate them from other students of color. This choice erases Asian American students in the district who face poverty, language barriers, higher rates of discipline, and lower rates of graduation than their White peers, and these students get left out of supportive services as a result. In Washington's Bellevue School District, Asian American students make up over 40 percent of the district, yet none of the required books in the district's middle school language arts curriculum were by Asian authors, and Asian students are nearly absent from the district's equity reports and goals.[29]

In the contentious debate over achievement, belonging, and representation in education, I posit that we've been asking the wrong questions altogether. What do numbers and accomplishments signify when others continue to frame and write our narratives, deciding how we're counted and represented, without fully respecting our subjectivities? What is overrepresentation without institutional or cultural power to influence how AAPIs are centered, or even considered, in decisions, policy, and practice in education? Debates on representation in institutions assume that we should assess disadvantaged status by the extent of numerical underrepresentation in a privileged institution, but statistical representation is not the best measure of discrimination. Representational parity in an institution does not imply equitable access, racial progress, or the dismantling of White dominance. In the case of Chinese Americans in higher education, we witnessed how insidiously White interest groups co-opted our stories and identities to protect White interests in anti–affirmative action lawsuits.

Racialization of Asian Americans is too complex to be reduced to numbers of undergraduate college students. Can we really substantiate claims of success through numerical increases in representation, when the categories to measure such representation are limited, stereotypical, and erase several Asian and Pacific Islander subgroups? I'm not arguing that we should not consider statistical underrepresentation as a sign that discrimination is present. In fact, underrepresentation is informative and central to the discussion on racial progress, and the underrepresentation of Southeast Asians and Pacific Islanders motivates this argument altogether. Further, the devastating 2023 Supreme Court decision dismantling affirmative action begs us to continue counting and fighting for fair representation in higher education. At the same time, there's more to measure *in addition* to numerical representation, especially for Asian Americans who occupy slippery, fickle racial positions in the racial hierarchy and encapsulate so many diverse subgroups. Statistical representation should not be the only measure of racial progress. After all, our "overrepresentation" has hardly shifted power in PWIs away from Whiteness. PWI-WAAs are still PWIs.

Statistical parity feels like an incomplete policy goal, and was not even the fundamental aim of affirmative action. Its original purpose was to ban discrimination and ensure equal opportunity, but this gets confounding for Asian Americans, who are simultaneously overrepresented and excluded. Our status as people of color and our multifold experiences with racial discrimination can't be fully captured by the statistical representation framework, which begs us to ask a new set of questions altogether. Instead of solely measuring numerically, we should qualitatively assess access (or lack of access) to power. Alleged overrepresentation in educational and professional spheres does not mean affirmative action no longer benefits Asian Americans, and proportional representation does not imply anti-Asian discrimination has ended.

As a Chinese American in academia, I'm supposedly one of the more represented Asian subgroups. I see a lot of students who look like me on campus, yet I have no Asian American tenured professors in my department. Asian Americans are underrepresented in sociology and feel marginal in sociological research on race and racism. While I feel privileged as a first-generation college student to pursue a doctoral degree, I also feel like I'm fighting every day. Fighting to trust that I belong here, fighting to be seen as a legitimate scholar on the study of racism by an academic discipline that interprets me as White-adjacent, and fighting against the anti–affirmative action, color-blind racist logics that my community—Chinese Americans—has galvanized over.

As an early doctoral student, I was eager to contribute to a research team's study on beliefs and behaviors in mental health. The study's survey asked participants how they explained mental illness: as a result of social factors, biological factors, demon possession, or tests from God. Seeing the latter two options, I enthusiastically proposed a paper on how different Asian ethnic groups' beliefs about mental health impacted whether and where they sought out mental health services. I've heard my own family members deny depression or anxiety, but blame symptoms on a ghost or demon possession. And what can a psychiatrist possibly do about a ghost or demon? Because our cultural frameworks on mental health are often incongruent with Western training in psychiatry, mental illness is underdiagnosed and undertreated in our communities. How

Asian immigrant and refugee subgroups conceptualize mental health impacts the likelihood they get help, and the source of that help. If we gather research on the etiology of mental health among Laotian, Burmese, Korean, Filipino, and other Asian subgroups, we can better contextualize mental health outreach and interventions to fit specific cultural frameworks.

Upon my proposal, one of the lead research scientists explained that Asian American participants were 1) not disaggregated ethnically, and 2) statistically too insignificant in the study to even be meaningfully included. We would categorize them as "Other" with multiracial individuals. Black, White, Hispanic, and Other were the demographic labels the study used. No visibility of Asian Americans, and no mention of Indigenous populations, even though American Indian and Alaska Native groups had the highest suicide rates in 2021,[30] right before we conducted this study on mental health. These moments expose the futility of representation. Why does it matter that I, along with American Indian, Black, and Latino students, can access these departments, when we ultimately have minimal influence over how our communities are counted, categorized, and narrativized? We are ultimately trapped in a structure that refuses to see us unless we uphold White racial logics and its classifications.

Academics often advise PhD students like me to play by the rules, get published in academic journals, and achieve tenure first. Once I do that, *then* I can write freely, design the studies I want, and push back on disciplinary norms and boundaries. But from what I have seen, this is a process that takes decades, with no promise of tenure. And more often than not, the academic becomes pacified as she waits. We give up so much, not just time and labor, but agency over where we live and how we use our voice, as they dangle the possibility of faculty appointments, awards, validation, and belonging in front of us. They demand our productivity, reward our compliance, and punish us when we challenge the status quo. During the genocide of Palestinians, not a single faculty member at my institution signed on to the open letter of Sociologists in Solidarity with Gaza. I witness too many academics decoupled from the radical politics and aspirations they once might have held because they are afraid to destabilize the institutional power they've sacrificed so much to secure. But is institutional power that traps you into silence actually power at all?

I refuse to struggle for these institutions to accept me if my acceptance muzzles me from speaking freely about the urgent issues of our day that demand my public advocacy and scholarly attention. I reject inclusion into PWIs as the ultimate, precious thing to protect. I decline to fight for my place in an institution that only uses me to uphold color-blind "diversity" and anti-Black mythologies of achievement. Instead, our community, expansive in its heterogeneity, is the beloved body I protect and struggle with. I don't know what comes next post–affirmative action, but I implore those of us in these institutions to abandon the aspiration to be seen and beloved by them. These institutions will never love us back.

Instead, I aspire for us as Asian Americans, especially those of us in PWIs of any kind, in any industry, to threaten the Whiteness of these spaces visibly, disruptively, and dangerously. May we refuse to be used by Whiteness, but leverage our "disproportionate" numbers to be unassimilable.

Blackface at UCI

April 2013, Lambda Theta Delta (LTD), the largest and oldest Asian fraternity at UC Irvine, posted a music video of its members singing a Justin Timberlake and Jay-Z song, with the member depicting Jay-Z in blackface.

LTD PRESENTS...

SUIT AND TIE

"No racism intended. All fun and laughter."

145K views

While I've never been part of Greek life, I can appreciate when nonWhite groups create their own spaces in traditionally White structures.

But in creating their own Asian fraternity, LTD assimilated into the time honored, racist tradition of blackface, which White fraternities have historically been enthusiastic practitioners of.

Blackface scandal at lambda chi alpha

"compton cookout" racist frat party mocks black history month

In a traditionally White space, Asian Americans used blackface to:

Establish their racial status as definitively NOT BLACK

Endorse the anti-Black racial order

... Regardless of whether racism was "intended."

"What was more American than blackface minstrelsy?"

"Like lynching, blackface minstrelsy is made possible by what Frank Wilderson describes as the Black's 'infinite and indeterminately horrifying and open vulnerability to violence.'"

Claire Jean Kim, author of
Asian Americans in an Anti-Black World

Asian Americans who do blackface labor to prove that they, like Whites, are the ones violating, not the ones being violated

145K views

If this is how we carve out our own spaces in White institutions, I don't want it.

3
Church Camp

The summer before ninth grade, one of my best friends at Westridge, Valerie, invited me into her secret world of church. I had no idea Valerie and her fancy private school family in Pasadena had an entire support system and social life at First Chinese Baptist Church (FCBC) in Los Angeles's Chinatown. Valerie was quiet and shy at school; she only opened up to a few of us. But at church, she was popular and vivacious, and didn't stop talking. FCBC's youth service was a whole production with a live band, stage lights, college students who were "youth counselors," and well-dressed Chinese American teenagers greeting you at the door with leaflets containing church announcements and social events for the week.

After the initial visit, I begged my parents to let me keep going, and eventually to attend their summer church camp. My parents were wary but obliged, only because they knew Valerie's family weren't cult leaders. By the second week of August, early on Monday morning, as the sun was still rising, I joined hundreds of Chinese American youth in the FCBC parking lot. With the polluted smells and sounds of the 110 freeway encroaching beside us, we loaded our backpacks and sleeping bags onto charter buses, which drove us out of the city, through the winding, carsickness-inducing mountain roads, into the verdant campgrounds of Big Bear.

Valerie got on the bus first and sat next to her church bestie, Jennifer, and I got shuffled into a seat behind them, next to a four-foot-ten, sassy ninth grader named Kimberly. Kimberly wore basketball shorts and basketball shorts only. She spoke loud and fast, berated boys, and was beloved and feared by all. She was the coolest person I had ever met. She was standoffish at the beginning of our ride, until I noticed her lunch bag said SAN GABRIEL VALLEY on it.

"I'm from San Gabriel too!"

"What! No, you're not. You go to school with Valerie."

"I do, but I live in San Gabriel!"

"What street do you live on, then?"

"Camden Avenue."

"I could walk there! I live by the fire station down Del Mar, on Thirty-Eighth Street."

"With the creepy, haunted park, right?"

"The Vincent Lugo Park ghosts!"

"Wow, we're basically neighbors, us and the ghosts."

Kimberly and I bonded instantly. I befriended someone who understood me in a different way, simply because we shared the same ethnoburb zip code. I was struck by this Chinese American ecosystem that felt like home, even while the religious aspects were foreign to me. The magic of church camp was enchanting, as I spent the next five days learning to sing "How Great Is Our God" (Chris Tomlin version, White evangelical icon of the 2000s), participating in ropes courses and scavenger hunts, and shouting church camp chants in the dining hall with new friends designated as my "grade." I was in the woods for the first time, with other youth and adults who looked like me, encountering God in and through this intentional, protected, ethnic-specific space, through shared religious and social activities.

In his 1912 volume *The Elementary Forms of Religious Life*, French classical sociologist Émile Durkheim describes what I experienced at church camp as "collective effervescence." According to Durkheim, individuals create, experience, and release a certain "electricity" through accumulated moments in social life where they perform religious rituals together. This social sharing of emotions through ritual transports individuals outside of themselves, leading to a communal emotional excitement or delirium. Sociologist Russell Jeung argues that the ecstasy of rituals, music, communion, and prayers in ethnic and pan-Asian churches work together to create and affirm not just religious belonging but ethnic and Asian American group identity.[1]

The collective effervescence of church camp was certainly spellbinding, because it became my gateway drug to the next ten years in evangelicalism. I immediately started going to church three times a week and became a full-fledged Jesus freak. I was feral for my church community. My church friends all lived in the ethnoburb, within ten minutes from me, and we made up excuses to see one another even more than we already did at church. I went from never having gone to church or thought about God at all to zealous weekly worship, Sunday school attendance, youth group, scripture reading, morning prayer, and even baptism in ninth grade, when I got dunked in a pool. After church services, my church friends and I spent Sunday afternoons gallivanting around Chinatown, before Chinatown became gentrified by White-owned art galleries and sommelier storefronts. We frequented local Chinese businesses for five-dollar lunches with a kind of independence that I didn't yet have in the car-centric ethnoburb. When a junior asked me to prom through a public promposal in the church gym, I felt like FCBC royalty.

Unlike my White teachers at Westridge, adults at church saw leadership potential in me. I was invited to teach in children's ministry and facilitate Bible studies with my peers. My youth group counselors encouraged me to explore my interest in faith and social justice, and even invited me to preach at my youth group about "God's heart for the poor." I took on every single leadership role available, received mentorship from counselors and Sunday school teachers, and got involved in theater ministry, getting cast in church plays for Easter and Christmas services. Unlike my glamorous pursuit of the stage at Westridge, where I was cast once in *Cabaret* as a nameless extra with no lines, I played dynamic, complex main characters in our church plays. At FCBC, I was no longer in the background.

I got baptized into not only the church community but its theologies, which would come to shape my consciousness and self-perception during my formative adolescent years. I began to see myself almost exclusively through the lens of FCBC's conservative evangelical teachings. In his 1903 seminal work *The Souls of Black Folk*, W. E. B. Du Bois defined "double consciousness" as the sense of "two-ness" Black Americans experience because of racial oppression and their devalued place in White society, whereby they are "always looking at one's self through the eyes of others." Double consciousness is not a benign internal state of being but a psychic danger by which Black Americans, under the violence of Jim Crow and "the color line," measure themselves by standards that always uphold and privilege Whiteness. Double consciousness reflects two unreconciled souls, defined and torn by the dehumanizing ways Blackness is perceived by the White gaze. My fragmented lives in the ethnoburb and my PWI lent themselves to a milder version of my own double consciousness, which would soon fracture into a triple consciousness as I began to measure myself by the standards set by the church.

Immersing myself fully into FCBC also meant internalizing their legalistic, often literal interpretations of the Bible. I came to understand and judge myself by what FCBC defined as good and holy. I assimilated into the church's bifurcated ideas of the sacred and profane and rigid notions of saved and heathen, and my internalization of heterosexist purity culture was one of the clearest costs of this. I sincerely believed myself to be inherently sinful because I questioned my sexuality. I would stay up late every night crying to Jesus to heal me from my "lust." They taught me that I was broken, and I believed it. They also taught me that through Jesus, I could be saved, become good, and give my life meaning, and I believed that too. As an Asian American youth at a PWI, my Chinese church gave me a sense of home and community. I was convinced I needed to fiercely obey their teachings, particularly around gender and sexuality, to protect the belonging I found there. While FCBC became a site for my fragmented selves in the ethnoburb and PWI to come together, it also further dismembered me.

In historian Kathryn Gin Lum's *Heathen: Religion and Race in American History*, religion played a central role in constructing the White gaze, intersected with categories of oppression, specifically race, gender, and sexuality. Religion—expressed through White Christian conquest—is another dimension of double consciousness, and part of the "psychic danger" through which non-White people view themselves. In Lum's research, White Christian Protestants who arrived in and colonized North America understood "heathens" as anybody non-White and outside of Abrahamic religious traditions. Heathens presumably didn't know how to take care of their own bodies or lands, and needed Christians to help. This classification justified missionary and colonial conquests to fulfill the Great Commission's charge to "make disciples of all nations." Lum writes, "Classifying people as heathen served as a ticket of impunity to justify taking over their lands, enslaving and reconstructing their bodies in the name of saving their souls."[2]

Through conversion into Christianity, Native Americans, Africans, and Asians would supposedly become Christianized and Americanized. Minister Josiah Strong, writing for the American Home Missionary Society in 1885, declared that these "feeble" races must "assimilate or die."[3] The notion that America is the spreader of salvation is not exclusive to White Protestant Americans, as non-White Christian converts would also come to view ancestors and unconverted relatives and friends through this violent White Christian gaze: as heathen and needing to be saved and assimilated. Perhaps one of the most dangerous consequences of colonialism, our own communities would come to internalize the fiction that Protestantism was the superior religion of the superior race.

The construction of religious righteousness and heathenism is essential to racial categories and dominance, defining the American racial state and justifying both exclusion and inclusion into the body politic. While some ministers saw the arrival of early Chinese immigrants as an opportunity to convert them, others argued for immigration restrictions to keep America from becoming heathenized. Lum describes the latter as the Great Omission, justifying immigration restrictions and racist violence. Proponents of exclusion proclaimed that Chinese laborers were willing to live on next to nothing, crowding into tenements in Chinatown and making meals from rats. They argued that Chinese heathen religion taught immigrants to devote all their energy and earnings to dead ancestors and neglect their living, bringing down the quality of life wherever they went. Religion was at the heart of racist logic as anti-Chinese hate and exclusion took violent forms. White Christian Protestants used religion to construct "the unassimilable Chinese." Even Reverend Father Buchard, a prominent Jesuit priest, characterized Chinese populations in San Francisco as "incapable of rising to the virtue that is inculcated by the religion of Jesus Christ."[4] Over time, even if converted, the Chinese heathen is always playing catch up with the White Christian.

Christian churches, including ethnic churches, became sites to simultaneously convert and assimilate the Chinese heathen. However, sociologist Fenggang Yang's *Chinese Christians in America: Conversion, Assimilation, and Adhesive Identities* demonstrates that over the years, the relationship between religion and assimilation has not been so unequivocal. While churches promoted the conversion and assimilation of

Chinese immigrants into mainstream American religious life, they also enabled Chinese Christians to preserve ethnic ties and strengthen ethnic solidarity around common experiences and cultural backgrounds. In these churches, Chinese Christians facilitated their own set of norms, rules, and boundaries of belonging.

FCBC began as a site to convert Chinese immigrants and integrate them into American society. FCBC held its first service in 1952 in a vacant noodle factory in Chinatown. A Los Angeles couple, Mr. and Mrs. Emory Chow, and a former Southern Baptist White missionary to China, Reverend M. W. Rankin, along with other ministers, established programs that served Chinese immigrants and their families at that time,[5] laying the foundation for decades of ministry to follow. As immigrants from Hong Kong and Taiwan poured into Chinatown and surrounding ethnoburbs after Hart–Celler, FCBC became a home church for them, eventually expanding and planting additional churches in surrounding ethnoburbs, including San Gabriel Valley, Westminster, and Walnut. While ethnic churches were assimilating institutions, FCBC also became an unassimilable space where Chinese immigrants and their descendants built community with co-ethnics and learned about God in their native languages.

While Christianity in the US has exclusionary, White supremacist roots and legacies, my faith and the church also saved me from the Whiteness of my adolescent years in private school. My teenage years with the Chinese church were part of a long legacy of immigrant churches supporting immigrants and their children. Historically, ethnic churches played an important role among immigrants and Black communities in the US. In *The Philadelphia Negro*, W. E. B. Du Bois high-lighted the role of the church as the center of Black social life, generating a sense of agency for enslaved and formerly en-slaved Black Americans. By operating as its own distinct Black social institution, the Black church was unassimilable and "unaffected" by the exploitative gaze and violence of the plan-tation system.[6] Among early White immigrant groups, ethnic churches helped them preserve their language and culture. The Italian Catholic parish, for example, functioned as a social institution organized around familiar religious and cultural symbols and shared identity.[7]

In line with this tradition, post-1965, Asian immigrant groups relied on ethnic congregations for social purposes, and the ethnic immigrant church emerged as its own distinct space to serve immigrant communities. The increase of Asian immigrants to the US as a result of Hart–Celler coincided with a nearly tenfold increase in ethnic churches from 1953 to 1984.[8] In fact, scholars note the church as its own ethnic enclave, facilitating close social ties with co-ethnics and repro-ducing the society of origin on a small scale.[9] While many Chinese immigrants converted,[10] groups like Koreans and Filipinos were often already religious and previously attended churches as sites of social gathering and spiritual formation in their home countries. Today, the church persists as a central space where Asian immigrants maintain and pass on ethnic culture and identity, preserve cultural traditions, and create co-ethnic social networks.[11]

Many of the churches that emerged in the last several decades were evangelical,[12] and post-1965 Asian immigrants were by far the biggest factor in the growth of Asian Amer-

ican evangelicalism.[13] The emergence of ethnoburbs provided a natural market for ethnic churches, and the growth
of evangelical ethnic churches was especially rapid among
post-1965 Korean and Chinese immigrants.[14] Many were
second-wave evangelicals, who first converted to Christianity
in Asia through American and other Western evangelical
organizations, denominations, and missions, while others
became evangelical after arriving in the US. In contrast to earlier generations of Asian immigrants and their descendants,
who gravitated toward mainline denominations, the post-1965
immigrants often preferred the decentralized nature of evangelical churches. Historian Jane Hong found that they were
wary of mainline denominations' emphasis on social justice
and engagement with contentious race and civil rights issues,
and embraced the more individualistic focus of evangelical
churches.[15] While the 1970s and 1980s birthed the religious
right in White evangelical history, transforming the relationship between religion and politics in the United States, the
1990s marked the growth of Asian American evangelicals.
By 2008, the proportion of Asian Americans identifying as
evangelical or born-again was 16 percent, which jumped to
25 percent in just four years in 2012.[16]

Biblical inerrancy, the belief that the Bible contains no
errors of any kind, is a central feature of American evangelicalism. Sociologist Antony Alumkal theorizes more recent
Asian immigrants are attracted to evangelicalism because
they may struggle with reconciling their ethnic identities
with their American identities, and may take comfort in the
fact that according to evangelicals, their true identities are
"in Christ."[17] The culturally and racially liminal space that

second-generation Asian Americans in particular occupy may heighten their need for certainty, priming them toward the definitiveness of evangelical theology.

In his study of Chinese American churches, Fenggang Yang similarly suggests that the unpredictability of the Chinese immigrant experience is one of the factors encouraging them to embrace evangelicalism:

> Living in this fast-changing, pluralistic, relativistic, and chaotic world, conservative Christians are assertive in proclaiming that the sole and absolute truth can only be found in the inerrant Bible. Evangelicals assure believers of absolute love and peace in this world and eternal life after death. For new Chinese immigrants, both premigration traumas and post-migration uncertainties in modern American society fortify their desire for absoluteness and certainty.[18]

In other words, evangelicalism offers community, credence, and even an escape from turbulent immigration experiences and uncertainty in the US racial landscape.

From my time at FCBC, I found this assurance of theological certainty salient among the second generation. Jennifer, Valerie's church bestie who attended FCBC since she was in her mother's womb, explained, "We really grew up at FCBC knowing the Bible. Our church has Southern Baptist roots, so our Sunday school teachers always made sure we were confident and absolute about our beliefs on things like homosexuality, abortion, and other important biblical issues." The perception that these issues are biblical, and the fixation on the Bible's clarity on them, gave Jennifer tools and comfort to navigate the world. While I was unsettled about the FCBC's hard-line reading of these "important biblical issues," I was attracted to the conviction and community that evangelicalism provided.

Since the 1990s, Asian Americans have made inroads and gained visibility in historically White evangelical institutions. The influx of Asian American college students into US parachurch groups such as InterVarsity Christian Fellowship (IVCF), for example, shifted religious life on college campuses. Asian Americans and Pacific Islanders made up 25 percent of attendees at IVCF's flagship evangelism conference, Urbana, in 1993; by 2012, they were 40 percent.[19] Even the Presbyterian Church of America (PCA) saw its Korean-language presbyteries, first created to be temporary in 1982, become the denomination's fastest-growing segment by the early 1990s.[20] Today, Christians are the largest single religious group within the Asian American community, and evangelicals have made up the majority of Asian American Christians since late 1970s to 1980s.[21] It's now unsurprising to see Asian Americans pastoring evangelical megachurches and leading seminaries, parachurch groups, and denominational organizations.[22]

While Asian Americans may find community in these evangelical spaces, these are also assimilating institutions. Even in ethnic churches, the racial politics of Whiteness persist. While her research is not on evangelicals, anthropologist Aihwa Ong's *Buddha Is Hiding: Refugees, Citizenship, the New America* provides a blueprint to contemplate the assimilating role of religion among Asian Americans. Ong studied the Mormon church as a site to facilitate Cambodian refugees' everyday processes of self-making and *being made* into "deserving" American citizen. Ong argues that poor Asian immigrants and refugees experience "a continuity of policy and practice that promotes 'ethnic cleansing,'" in the sense of removing the features of immigrants' supposedly primitive cultures that are socially determined "undesirable" so that they become eligible for American citizenry. The Mormon church works with state institutions like refugee camps, social workers, nurses, the police, and schools to assimilate non-White groups.

I'm not comparing my experience with evangelicals to that of Cambodian refugees in the Mormon church. However, Ong's framework helps identify evangelical churches and parachurch ministries as assimilating institutions for Asian Americans, paradoxically affirming ethnic identity while indoctrinating us into conservative conceptualizations of race and politics. In a 2020 study, second-generation Asian American evangelicals merged with White Christians in expressing some of the lowest support for equal opportunity.[23] Further, attendance at religious services is associated with higher rates of political participation, and for Asian American evangelicals in particular, with support for conservative politics and policies.[24] Asian American and Latino evangelicals are more likely to join the Republican Party than their co-ethnics, and more likely to support the conservative agenda of White evangelicals on issues of abortion and same-sex marriage.[25] In attitudes about immigrants hurting the economy and support for Black Lives Matter, Asian Americans who perceive in-group embattlement (belief that discrimination against Christians is a big problem) and that the American way of life needs to be protected are more conservative than those who do not.[26] Scholars suggest cultural assimilation among second-generation Asian American evangelical Christians explains their alignment with White evangelical racial attitudes and political views.[27] Evangelicalism is clearly at work in shaping views and votes on race and politics.

The distinct mono-ethnic makeup of ethnic churches also affects how Asian Americans conceptualize their own racial identities and understand racial difference. A study found that an immigrant-generation Chinese Protestant church shared sermons that contained the message that Chinese Christians are morally superior to both Chinese non-Christians and non-Chinese Christians.[28] Similarly, Korean American evangelicals in monoethnic churches are more likely than those in multiethnic churches to affirm the model minority stereotype and highlight racial and class boundaries between them and other racial groups. In *Korean American Evangelicals: New Models for Civic Life*, sociologist Elaine Howard Ecklund found that Korean Americans who participate in second-generation Korean churches use religion to largely reproduce images of Korean Americans as model minorities, and implicitly distance themselves from those whom they perceive as less financially successful. Contrastingly, Korean Americans in multiethnic congregations use religion to emphasize the commonality Korean Americans have with other minorities.

Evangelical ethnic churches not only facilitate racial boundaries and cultural citizenship, they utilize explicit and implicit spiritual violence through ideology, rituals, and politics to normalize heteropatriarchy and demonize queerness and non-Whiteness. Because of colonialism in Asia and Christianity being the dominant faith tradition in the United States, many Asian Americans who grow up in the evangelical church are inundated at an early age by the church's homophobic and heterosexist theology and practices, derived from early notions of "heathen." The discussion of sexuality and queerness in Asian American Christianity is not simply a theological debate but a piece of the larger historical context of normativity and subject-making through religion, culture, race, gender, sexuality, class, nation-state, and colonialism.

Before Christian missionaries arrived in Asia, Asian societies had their own social constructions of sexuality that were often affirming of sexual and gender fluidity, as documented in postcolonial feminist theologian Kwok Pui-Lan's work on precolonial literature and historical records. In China, homoerotic relationships of both men and women were accepted as long as they did not challenge the social hierarchy. In India, unions of same-sex love are described as the wedding of two souls in classical and canonical texts. In the Philippines, same-sex relations and gender expressions beyond the gender binary were common and bore no stigma.[29] There are bountiful accounts of queer desire and transgender expression in precolonial Asia, and they had their own words in their own languages to describe what we, in English, understand as queer and trans.

However, the cultural imperialist attitudes of Christian missionaries in Asia regarded these sexual practices of indigenous communities as symptoms of inferior "heathen" cultures. British and American colonial rule propagated monogamous heterosexual marriage as the norm by criminalizing homosexuality. Colonial fantasy also portrayed Asian men as soft, effeminate, and less masculine in comparison to the White heterosexual masculinity of colonizers.[30] Today, Western cultural imperialism continues to deploy gender stereotypes and homophobia to stigmatize communities, bodies, and behaviors that don't conform to the White heterosexual norm. This continues to determine the views of mainstream American churches, including ethnic churches, that understand queerness as deviant.

During the debates on sexuality in mainline churches throughout the 1980s and 1990s, institutions opposing the ordination and full inclusion of queer church members strategically cited the anti-gay stance of racial minority churches, pitting communities of color against queer people in church politics and society at large. Into the early 2000s, many Asian American church leaders treated homosexuality as a White, middle-class phenomenon, assuming it did not exist in our own community.[31] By 2008, during California's Proposition 8 banning gay and lesbian marriages, the Asian American vote was split and the church played a significant role. At this time, Asian Americans met and gathered together in church congregations more than any other type of community association. Korean and Filipino Americans currently still have the highest rates of church attendance out of any ethnic group in the US, and they disproportionately attend evangelical Protestant and Catholic churches,[32] which promoted Proposition 8. FCBC was eerily silent on all things political except for same-sex marriage. I recall petitions, "1 woman + 1 man" campaign T-shirts, and church service announcements urging congregants to vote yes on Proposition 8. Overall, 84 percent of weekly churchgoers voted yes on Prop 8,[33] and it can be assumed that Asian American church attendees voted similarly. More than ethnicity or age, religion was the key to influencing how Asian Americans voted on marriage equality.[34]

I WAS STILL A JESUS ENTHUSIAST BY THE TIME I WENT TO COL-lege, although a little less obnoxiously zealous. I at least stopped wearing my WWJD braided camp bracelet unironically. My Sunday school teachers worried about me moving so far from the safety of our ethnoburb, all the way to Oakland, where I wouldn't know anybody or have a Chinese church to fall back on. They expressed concerns about Mills College, where I would attend, for being so liberal and so gay and possibly turning me so liberal and so gay as well. My church mentors urged me to find an on-campus fellowship and church as soon as I got to Oakland, lest I lose my faith to the heathen lesbians in Birkenstocks.

I was thrilled to move away, but I also heeded their command to find the Christians on campus. My first week at school, I joined a group called Workers of Faith, the only on-campus Bible study. They were a quirky, nerdy, racially diverse group of about ten college students who talked about "social justice" and "racial reconciliation." They named their group after the Bible verse "faith without works is dead" in the book of James. Their group facilitator was an extremely pregnant, endearingly sassy Taiwanese American woman in her early thirties named Jia, who proclaimed things like "The income inequality in this country is jacked up," and "God wants to heal the injustices in our world and restore us back to *shalom*."

I wasn't sure what she was talking about, but I quickly bought in. The way Jia spoke about Jesus and social issues was captivating, and I'd found a community who shared my faith.

I diligently attended Bible study every Wednesday night, and eventually immersed myself in their group and their parent organization, InterVarsity Christian Fellowship. My first year at Mills College was a challenging transition for me, and this religious community became a source of comfort. I didn't quite know where I fit in socially on campus, I was lost in all the unstructured free time I suddenly had, and I missed the familiarity of Westridge and FCBC. I missed my PWI Asians and churchgoing ethnoburb Asians. The student body at Mills College was about 50 percent students of color, which is pretty impressive for a private, historically White institution, but there were very few Asian Americans. In my eyes at the time, the students of color were mostly Black and Brown, majored in Ethnic Studies, and passionately referenced Angela Davis, Audre Lorde, and other people I had never heard of. They seemed to always be telling everyone to "check their privilege." As an Asian American from the ethnoburb, I was intimidated. I was clueless about how to "check my privilege," and didn't know if or how I would fit in among this activist-oriented campus climate I suddenly found myself in. InterVarsity, on the other hand, was a space that felt socially safer and easier.

In October of my first year at Mills, I went to InterVarsity's fall conference, their annual retreat for students from different InterVarsity chapters across the San Francisco Bay Area. I encountered hundreds of East Asian students, many from ethnoburbs like SGV. Instead of the intense confrontations over race, class, and privilege I experienced on campus, InterVarsity was a space where we talked about our personal relationships with Jesus and a *spiritual* approach to social justice. The conference reminded me of home. Things felt simpler, as I temporarily escaped the challenging conversations on campus about racial identity and politics accosting my fragile ethnoburban heart.

InterVarsity became my spiritual and social home for not only the rest of my college years, but into my twenties. I gave so much time, money, labor, and emotional investment to this organization that my parents thought they lost me to a cult. I not only attended weekly Bible studies and retreats multiple times a year, I fundraised (also: defied all cultural and social norms by asking my friends and family for money) to attend their missions trips over multiple summers and work for them full-time as a campus minister after college. I wanted in on this mission-driven, faith-based organization. In addition to the community, I believed InterVarsity would give me leadership opportunities I thought I couldn't get elsewhere as a young Asian American woman, including invitations to teach, preach, and travel.

Perhaps most compelling, InterVarsity gave me a theological lens to understand the racial politics I encountered at Mills and in Oakland at the time, selling me on a vision of becoming a "world changer" in this confusing, violent world I was coming into adulthood in. Halfway into my freshman year at Mills, Oscar Grant was murdered on New Year's Day by Officer Johannes Mehserle at Fruitvale Station, about ten minutes from my campus. Fruitvale Station was our BART stop. My friends and I would park and ride the train from Fruitvale into

San Francisco for our freshman-year adventures. Fruitvale Station was also home to a predominantly Latino community, with taco trucks, fruit stands, the Fruitvale library, and families, commuters, cyclists, and pedestrians passing through every day. I could not process how this horrifying public execution could happen at a location so mundane and familiar to me. Overnight, Fruitvale Station became the historic site of the police murder of a Black man that galvanized the city and country.

Protests erupted in Oakland throughout my spring semester, and many Black students at Mills took to the streets to join the community to protest the unjust killing. I watched the video of the shooting, where Grant is already pinned down, handcuffed, and helpless moments before he is shot to death. I learned that Grant was only twenty-two, was unarmed, and had a young daughter. I witnessed and empathized with the collective indignation on the streets. As I read and listened to the historically situated laments of my Black peers and neighbors, their grief penetrated the sheltered naiveté of my heart. But outwardly, I mostly stayed silent. I didn't know how to channel my accumulating grief. I wanted to support Black students on campus, yet I didn't feel like I had a place or the authority to show up to any of the conversations, town halls, or actions. I felt strongly about this public lynching captured on camera and circulated on early social media, but my fear of not knowing how to show up correctly kept me from tangibly showing up at all.

Mehserle's trial began the following summer, when I was on an "urban missions project" in Oakland with InterVarsity. I attended this six-week immersive program with hopes that it could give me answers as I learned about our country's fraught racial history, and Oakland's unique place in it. That summer, I, along with five other college students from across the Bay Area, lived in West Oakland and ran a summer camp for children in the neighborhood. An "urban missions trip" feels colonial, and in many ways it was. Our program director assigned us readings from the Bible and books written by White Christians about racial justice. I was essentially volun-touring a historically divested neighborhood to "learn about Jesus and justice." Looking back, anything helpful I learned was from my relationships with community members. As we partnered with community-based organizations to provide free breakfast on Saturdays, I learned from my neighbors about the Black Panthers who ran the Free Breakfast Program on the same block. As we approached Mehserle's trial that summer, community members and neighbors helped me understand the gravity and implications of the case.

Mehserle was found guilty of involuntary manslaughter and not guilty of voluntary manslaughter and second-degree murder. He was sentenced to two years for murdering Oscar Grant, and was released under parole after serving only eleven months. I was volunteering at an optometry clinic on our block at the time the media released the verdict, and the entire neighborhood fell quiet. A cloud of disappointment and indignation, familiar to the neighborhood but new to me, overcame us. My heart broke and expanded in ways my consciousness did not yet have the categories to hold or understand. The color-blind racist ideology from the 2010s left me ill-prepared to make sense of what was happening in the streets, in the West Oakland community, and among my neighbors. I grew even more confused as the media hyperfixated on the damages and property destruction of the protests. I didn't get why protestors shut down freeways and broke the windows of Chase Bank, only to have janitorial staff clean it up afterward. Ignorant of the symbolic and material implications of these actions, I bought into the mainstream narrative that these protesters were causing more harm than helping. I didn't yet understand the power and necessity of shutting it down.

That summer, InterVarsity fed me a lens to understand these events, selling me on a theological vision of what I could do about the intensity I witnessed and felt. My program leaders explained the racial violence and subsequent protests as "broken shalom": broken relationship between humanity and God. Racial injustice was a spiritual issue, resulting from humanity's separation from God. Because we, as humanity, are separated from God, we are also separated from one another, thus explaining the racist violence and tension we witnessed that summer.

The lessons InterVarsity taught me about racism and social injustice reflect what sociologists describe as White evangelicalism's religio-cultural scripts on inequality. In the dominant White evangelical framework, suffering and injustice are not understood as institutional and structural issues, but as individual and interpersonal concerns. They believe the root of all social problems is sin, affecting individuals and corrupting relationships between us.[35] InterVarsity taught us that racial violence, looting and property destruction, and the historical divestment from West Oakland as a historically Black neighborhood are all results of sin, rather than effects of and responses to structural failures of our state. Instead of confronting unfair laws or unjust institutional behaviors, they presented and idealized interpersonal reconciliation as the solution to injustice. In hyperprioritizing the individual and interpersonal, we neglected to consider how interpersonal relationships and individual agency are conditioned by social structures such as policy, discrimination, and segregation.

Given this framework, InterVarsity, like many evangelical churches and ministries, directed us to address racial inequality through racial reconciliation theologies.[36] Because racism is framed as primarily a spiritual problem, it demands spiritual solutions, including repentance, forgiveness, and unity through a common identity "in Christ."[37] The evangelical racial reconciliation framework downplays political action in addressing race relations, instead emphasizing individuals pursuing relationships across racial lines. They held a suspicion toward institutional explanations and solutions for social problems, because how could changing laws change our sinful hearts? They believed the problem of racism is not located in society's structures but in the individual and interpersonal, so the solutions must also be individual, interpersonal, and nonstructural.

Looking to Christ as the ultimate and only reconciliatory solution to racism, sociologist Michelle Oyakawa asserts that racial reconciliation theologies function as a suppressive frame, precluding discussions about racial inequality and discouraging collective action to promote racial justice. This focus on interpersonal and nonstructural solutions, such as cross-racial friendship building, explains how evangelicals can decry racial inequality while also promoting solutions that do not address the source of the structural problem.[38] For example, while the Southern Baptist Convention called for members to declare "Black Lives Matter" in June 2020, responding to the murder of George Floyd and subsequent protests, evangelicals overwhelmingly demotivated systemic interventions to racial violence. This lens may support formal legal equality for members of different races, but oppose programs to defund the police or implement affirmative action, designed to directly address racial inequality and redistribute economic and political resources.

I was attracted to InterVarsity's racial frameworks because they gave me a sense of agency. The racial reconciliation theology provided me the fantasy of control over these larger issues that otherwise made me feel powerless. If I could get right with God and the people in my life, and teach others to do the same, I could be antiracist. The reductive simplicity of White evangelical theologies on race, centering the individual and interpersonal, provided me an escape from harder questions about my Asian American identity as I navigated racial politics at Mills and in Oakland. I wouldn't have to reflect on or address how I benefited from and contributed to systems of racism, because racism isn't systemic, it's interpersonal! What a relief. I wouldn't have to think about my racial positionality as an Asian American, or my historical and individual relationships with Black, Brown, and White communities. I just had to think about Jesus, repent from sin, and live "right" with other people, whatever that meant. Evangelicalism was escapism.

As the Black Lives Matter movement brought increasing national attention to police brutality and anti-Blackness throughout the 2010s, racial reconciliation theologies could not hold up. The state of the world pulled me to outgrow these reductive frameworks. Eric Garner, Philando Castile, Mike Brown, Alton Sterling, the list goes on, were not killed "because of sin." There was something deeper operating, a profound moral failing embedded in the White supremacist foundation of our nation and its institutions that was inadvertently upheld by my lack of critical analysis. My simplistic spiritual and racial frameworks failed me, but I continued to stay with InterVarsity because several of us started interrogating, unlearning, and resisting these interpretations. Jia ended up becoming my mentor, and gathered a small group of us within InterVarsity to initiate faith-based advocacy projects, like raising Oakland's minimum wage, or partnering with Black churches and civic organizations to march to Sacramento to lobby on behalf of police reform initiatives. Slowly but surely, our faith and growing criticality demanded we consider systemic solutions to the problems we witnessed.

Jia created a niche within InterVarsity that approached social justice from spiritual, structural, and activist orientations. Her faith-based organizing helped me connect current events, history, and policy to my spirituality, but our programs always felt inferior to the larger evangelical organization. In national InterVarsity gatherings, our emphasis on and structural approach to social justice were marginalized. Other InterVarsity staff, especially those who were East Asian, seemed embarrassed of us. They criticized us for being "too extreme," "ungracious," and "impatient." Authority figures implored us to "focus on the gospel" and stop depressing the students. Instead of justice-oriented ministry, they wanted us to buy into and sell "multiethnicity": their vision of diverse

Christians living harmoniously with one another, without addressing the material inequalities among/within us and our communities. I felt the pressure to assimilate to this agenda from InterVarsity superiors and peers every time we gathered. From passive-aggressively shaming us, to explicitly telling us to "tone down" our curriculum, the message was to abide by their White evangelical frameworks on race.

Many East Asians in InterVarsity were seen (and saw themselves) as revolutionary leaders in the organization, paving the way for younger Asian Americans like me to feel belonging within evangelicalism. I gave so much of myself to InterVarsity in part because of these leaders and elders in the organization, serving as examples of what my future in evangelical ministry could look like. And yet, here they were, demanding to see and "edit" my sermon notes before I spoke, a hurdle I never saw them put others through. These East Asian leaders were the ones who directed me to make myself more palatable to evangelicals, and to remove words like "heteropatriarchy" from my sermons because InterVarsity "was not ready." I was unprepared for this type of censorship from people who claimed to be my "spiritual family." Finding and worshiping with people who looked like me, with similar backgrounds, was what drew me to Christianity in the first place. And now, "my people" were the ones demanding I dilute myself, leaving White racial logics in the organization unchallenged.

Around this time, Jia and I began hearing rumors of InterVarsity's forthcoming "theological position and policy on human sexuality." Until then, I generally had the flexibility to teach what I wanted on campus. Even though I wasn't ordained, I quickly learned how radical it was for me, in a position of spiritual authority, to welcome queer, trans, and questioning young adults into our Bible study. This is the bare minimum, but unfortunately, something rarely experienced by queer and trans students. It became glaringly important for me to use my role as a campus minister to affirm these students, and to provide a safe space for questioning students to explore spirituality and sexuality. In InterVarsity conferences, I created breakout groups for queer students across the Bay Area to gather. These spaces explicitly affirmed them as legitimate, both as Christians and as queer people. The rumors about InterVarsity's forthcoming policy threw me, disrupting what became my vocational purpose, my evolving theological beliefs, and soon, my own sense of self and sexual identity.

Only during InterVarsity's policy rollout did I begin to confront my queerness, and I questioned my own legitimacy. I doubted I was actually queer enough to take on these labels or have a real stake in these conversations about sexuality with InterVarsity. There were no categories or words that felt like enough. Through the deconstructing I did with my queer students around the Bible, gender, and sexuality, I began to understand sexuality not as a binary, or even as a spectrum, but as a constellation of possibilities of attractions and desires and love, in defiance of assumed and compulsory heterosexuality. Our communal unlearning pulled me out of the weight of InterVarsity's theological policy rollout to a place of freedom and self-acceptance. Our queer community saved me from evangelicalism.

As more students came out to me throughout my time with InterVarsity, especially those who were Asian American, they helped me grow more certain about my own queerness and bisexuality. In their confusion and questions, their worries about disappointing their parents and not being queer, Christian, or Asian enough, they still asserted and actualized who they knew themselves to be. I began to wonder if questioning is perhaps inherent to queerness, and panicking about legitimacy is universal to people who hold intersectional, often stigmatized, identities. With these shared experiences, they gave me language to articulate my own queerness and courage to trust what I know of myself. As Christian heterosexual norms and broader societal bi-invisibility tried to assimilate me into heterosexuality, I fought to resist, to become unassimilable, and to own my queer reality. I began to affirm myself.

I tried to share my journey with trusted colleagues in InterVarsity, but my evangelical coworkers were not ready to talk about the "constellation of queer possibility." Most of them empathized, but reminded me, "It's still a sin." I became hypervigilant as my so-called mentors and friends subtly, but consistently, tried to push me back into the reductive frame of debating theological beliefs when I simply wanted to share my lived experience. They would respond with scripture, doctrine, and definitions, and I would start noticing my own heart palpitations, sweating, sometimes trembling and shaking, and eventually chronic back pain that plagued me for a year. They discussed ideas, as my mind disassociated and my body paid the cost.

Asian American theologian Reverend Dr. Patrick Cheng uses Judges 19, an Old Testament story, as foundational text to write about the embodied realities of the queer Asian American Christian experience and to construct a queer Asian American biblical hermeneutic. In the biblical story he references, an unnamed concubine is "captured, betrayed, raped, tortured, murdered, dismembered, and scattered." It has been described as one of the most distressing and disturbing stories in the entire Bible. The unnamed concubine is read as a sexual outsider and a woman who is powerless, without "name, speech, or power." She is alone in a world of heteropatriarchy. She is also a geographical outsider, indigenous to a southern region but displaced to the north, where she is abused. Like the unnamed concubine, Cheng claims that queer Asian Americans are radical outsiders in our sexualities and geographies, in the diaspora, and marginal to heteronormativity.[39] The story ends with the unnamed concubine literally being dismembered. Her body is cut "limb by limb, into twelve parts," and scattered.

In his analysis, Cheng argues that queer Asian Americans experience multiple fragmentation as they negotiate which "part" of themselves is operative in a given context. Multiple fragmentation is a common theme in queer Asian American poetry and literature, and Cheng proposes that the multiple fragmentation and scattering of queer Asian Americans defuses the threat of our radical outsider existence. I constantly negotiated which "part" of myself was operative in InterVarsity. I did this to keep myself safe, and to lessen the threat and discomfort I posed to my coworkers when I questioned their policies and theologies. I longed for alignment and integration in my sexual, ethnic, and spiritual identities and lives, but this was not possible as long as I stayed in InterVarsity, where my full humanity was flattened to theological debates. While InterVarsity was once my community, it devolved into one I found myself alone in and an outsider to.

I struggled to find my way out of evangelicalism and, as a first step, attended a queer-affirming conference for LGBTQ+ Christians and allies. On the last night of the conference, I randomly encountered a multigenerational table of Asian Americans at our conference hotel, from youth to elders. I went to the conference knowing hardly anybody and had planned to eat by myself, but this table of Asian Americans eagerly waved me down to go sit with them. Their aggressive hospitality reminded me of FCBC. In fact, they looked like a post–Sunday service lunch hang, loud and loitering and unmovable. I was simultaneously intrigued and triggered.

As I sat at this table of familiar strangers, I learned that they were part of Evergreen Baptist, a traditionally conservative Chinese immigrant church that recently became queer-affirming. I ate with their queer youth, queer-affirming pastors, and several elders who attended the conference because they simply wanted to learn. I sat across from an older woman in her sixties. She spoke in a thick Cantonese accent about how she had failed to accept her daughter when she came out to her decades ago. She was now trying to repair their relationship, but had been pained with remorse for having let her theological beliefs rob them of so many years together. As I listened to her story, I felt grief for her and her daughter, and at the same time, strangely comforted. I don't expect to ever hear my former friends from Inter-Varsity or FCBC apologize and admit, "We were wrong." But now, sitting across from me, was this auntie who once held the same destructive beliefs as they did, admitting she was wrong. Her regret was validating, and her estrangement from her daughter was cruelly comforting because it reflected my own estrangement from my spiritual community.

We somehow found each other and, at least for a moment, were a little less isolated. Maybe I reminded her of her daughter, because she and her friends surely reminded me of the aunties at FCBC, who I had to break ties with once I came out. As I got to know different members of their church over this seren-dipitous meal, they provided a hospitality that felt like home, and expressed a sense of deep remorse and repentance that maybe felt close to justice. Their church's transformation and my healing became intertwined.

Today, I feel mostly ambivalent about church to protect myself from further disappointment. I keep my distance, but evangelicals, God, and the ethnic church in particular some-how continue to find me. My first summer in Houston, I wit-nessed my mother-in-law gather dozens of church ladies from their evangelical Filipino congregation to pull together a last-minute bridal shower for her niece Mary, who lost her mom when she was young. The church ladies barely knew Mary, and many of them met her for the first time at her own bridal shower, yet they all took on the role of chosen family. Preparing lechon and pancit, bridal party games, a photo booth, and a corner of the room full of gifts for the couple to start their new lives, these titas stepped up to serve as surrogate mothers. They blessed and celebrated this young woman, making sure she had maternal support for her big day.

This is what Asian churches do. They fill in the gaps for one another. There is no community care like a church meal train after a congregant gives birth or loses a family member. I've seen church members cover one another's hospital bills, provide housing and jobs, offer child care, and even sponsor one another's visas to immigrate. The Asian immigrant church is the most socialist site I've ever witnessed. When working for InterVarsity, I had to fundraise my living expenses as well as the costs of operating my ministry, and it was FCBC that made that happen. There is an unspoken expectation to take care of one another inherently embedded in Asian ethnic churches. It's our cultural value for interconnectedness and interdependence that gets put on overdrive in an immigrant church, where everyone's needs are understood and provided for. The ethnic church remains a refuge and a resource in a world where we are otherwise othered by Whiteness.

I miss it. I want to be part of this type of community again and raise my family in it. I want my child to be part of the intergenerational care, the meal trains, the youth groups, and the larger village of ates and jejes and titas and yi-yis and lolas and popos. And at the same time, I am done with these spaces. The Sunday after the bridal shower, their pastor preached an anti-immigrant sermon about entering the country "the right way" to his predominantly immigrant congregation, several of whom are undocumented. The cognitive dissonance feels too heavy. The radical, socialist care of the Asian church alongside its violent, carceral theologies are irreconcilable to me.

In my doctoral program, I spent extensive time at a Chinese immigrant evangelical church in Houston, very similar to FCBC, to conduct research. It shocked me how seamlessly I fit in. Like putting on evangelical cosplay, I brought my partner because I knew heterosexual attachment to a man would legitimize my presence. I knew what worship songs to expect (they're still singing "Oceans" by Hillsong), to use language like "discipleship" and "missional" and "loving on our neighbors," and how to speak with deference and stand behind my partner as I asked the male pastors for permission to interview their congregants. I knew how and what to hide: my politics, my queerness, my ambivalent faith. I easily induced this Chinese immigrant church persona again, making myself nauseous in the process. My triple consciousness activated as I shrank myself to be palatable to the Asian evangelical gaze. Because I'm not out to my husband's evangelical family, I find myself employing this persona with my family as well. I hide behind the fake agreeable and apolitical self, even if it's a facade, because I can't risk losing another community again.

As unassimilable and radical as these immigrant religious sites are, they also reproduce limited, racist frameworks and erect violent, heterosexist, patriarchal boundaries of belonging. My membership in these spaces, and among evangelical family members, feels conditional to my agreeability. These spaces are dialectic, simultaneously helping us survive Whiteness while converting us into the politics of Whiteness. I don't know if these spaces are redeemable to me, and I don't know if they can ever feel safe to me. And yet, as much as I want to refuse them, they continue to feel like home.

WHAT I MISS

Asian church potluck

  Church babies

Church music (even "Oceans")

Built-in community

How can I pray for you?

WHAT I LOVE

4

Racially Nowhere and Everywhere

I was working at my alma mater, Mills College, when the demonstrations in Ferguson began, protesting the police murder of Michael Brown on August 9, 2014. As racial consciousness of police brutality rose across the country, a student posted anonymously on a campus-wide messaging page, "All Black women at Mills should be lynched." That was the entire message. It was taken down shortly after, but the harm had already been inflicted. I stopped in my tracks as one of my students relayed this news to me.

Police officer Darren Wilson pursued and shot eighteen-year-old Michael Brown for "walking down the middle of the street, blocking traffic." Wilson fired twelve rounds, six of which hit and killed Brown. For four hours, the police ruthlessly left Brown's body in the summer heat. This horrific delay fueled public outrage: "It was very disrespectful to the community and the people who live there. It also sent the message from law enforcement that 'We can do this to you any day, any time, in broad daylight, and there's nothing you can do about it,'" said Patricia Bynes, a committeewoman in Ferguson.[1] I imagined the horror Brown's family, friends, and neighborhood must have felt, especially during those four hours. Activists have compared viral video footage of police killings of Black men to public lynchings, and this public disregard for Brown's body felt no different.

During subsequent protests, militarized police tear-gassed, fired rubber bullets at, and inflicted extreme force on protestors in Ferguson, most of whom were Black youth. Armored vehicles, shotguns, rubber-coated metal pellets, tear gas, and M4 rifles like those used by forces in Iraq and Afghanistan became a dystopian yet common sight. In a show of force, the militarized response made it clear that the state viewed the community protestors as the enemy. I saw the failures and violence of institutions that I previously presumed to serve and protect us. I witnessed policing cause and exacerbate the collective indignation in Ferguson. As I read story after story of protestors caring for one another, providing immediate relief and first aid on the ground, and cultivating systems of care in the midst of crisis, I also read about cops instigating and escalating force, intimidating and surveilling the community. As I overheard, "The whole damn system is guilty as hell," on the streets of Oakland in solidarity with Ferguson, my former evangelical frameworks on race and racial reconciliation crumbled under this growing, hefty understanding of systemic racism. No amount of racial reconciliation that my religious context preached about could begin to confront the structural horrors of racial violence that conditioned the attacks we saw on Black lives and communities on full display in Ferguson.

The mass uprising around the murder of Michael Brown gave me language to understand the structural inequalities and institutional failures behind poverty, divestment, police brutality, and other social issues, but this violent comment posted on the Mills College Facebook page was home base. This was my alma mater, my workplace, and in many ways, the haven where I became an adult. And this wasn't a police officer; this was a fellow student. Mills was my hella queer and activist-oriented women's college, Oakland was my chosen city and the birthplace of the Black Panthers, and California, supposedly one of the most progressive states in the country, had always been my home. This was both political and suffocatingly personal.

According to the college's administration, the incident launched an FBI investigation, but they never followed up with us about the results. Within days, the college hosted a town hall where administrators, faculty, staff, and students discussed the incident and next steps. Black students took the mic lamenting not only this incident but years of anti-Black microaggressions and violence in classrooms, dormitories, and campus life. Amid their own fear and racial trauma on campus, Black students educated the rest of the Mills community about their experiences as Black women at a PWI. I quickly realized that this incident was part of a long history of structural and interpersonal anti-Blackness on our campus, a distinct feature of PWIs. Even though Mills praised itself as a socially progressive women's college, Black students consistently felt excluded, dehumanized, and policed on campus. I listened and empathized, and sometimes I panicked. I wondered if I, an alum and now a campus minister at this school, contributed to these collective grievances. I recalled how as a student, I didn't think much about the experiences of Black women at all, and maybe that was the problem. I wondered about my place in all of this as a non-Black person of color.

My questions escalated as Amy, a Chinese American student in her third year at Mills, took the mic at the town hall. I remembered her from previous interactions as an eager student leader, overly involved in what seemed like every single extracurricular. I often found her tabling at club fairs promoting organizations, internships, or volunteer opportunities. She was enthusiastic, hurried, and spoke with a noticeable Chinese accent. Following the example of the Black women who spoke before her, Amy took the mic and shared her own experiences of victimization by White women on campus. "Stuff like this happens to Asians too! I've never felt like I belonged here! This is all an INJUSTICE!" she screeched into the mic. The microphone feedback resounded and we covered our ears. The whole room fell silent. I noticed the Black students stare at one another. Some were bewildered, while others rolled their eyes, exasperated. I was taken aback by how loud and emotional she was. While Asian Americans have historically been victimized by White supremacy, stuff like this *didn't* happen to us, right? I knew she meant well and I believed her experiences, but I also rarely found Mills College hostile. Sure, I experienced microaggressions, but unlike Black students on campus, I never had family members followed by campus security, and I never heard a student threaten me or my racial group as violently as we witnessed on the message board. In her signal of support, Amy's timing felt abrasive and dismissive of the Black women who were baring their souls before her. *This is not your moment*, I wanted to tell her. *And also, you're embarrassing me.*

In the midst of the Ferguson uprising and the campus incident, I began to study the myriad of ways Black and Asian experiences in this country were connected, but distinct. Hungry for historical context and language, I immersed myself in books, blogs, and community events where I learned about our different histories and experiences of racism. The "positive" stereotype of Asian Americans as the model minority depended on racist stereotypes of Black criminality, and ultimately served White conservative agendas. To address anti-Blackness, then, would also mean dismantling the model minority myth, disentangling ourselves from the grasp of White perception, and freeing ourselves to become more than the obedient immigrants they expected us to be. White supremacy needed these definitive, yet fictional narratives about Black and Asian people to maintain racial dominance and to divide and conquer. To move toward healing and coalition, we would have to acknowledge the different ways we've been victimized by White supremacy, but not conflate our experiences together.

Not all racial suffering is the same. In his article "People-of-Color-Blindness: Notes on the Afterlife of Slavery," author and political commentator Jared Sexton refers to this refusal to parse out the historical, social, subjective, and embodied differences among racial minorities as "people-of-color-blindness." While racial color-blindness implies the refusal to acknowledge a system of privileges and marginalization based on race, people-of-color-blindness refuses to acknowledge the systematic privileges and oppression that exist among different communities of color. Non-Black people of color, including Asian Americans, undoubtedly experience forms of structural violence. But according to Sexton, "It is the specific genealogy that links slavery to Jim Crow to the ghetto to the prison that warrants my claim about the singularity of racial domination of Blacks," and other racial minorities in America come out of "profoundly different historical processes and trajectories."[2] Similarly, cofounder of the Black Lives Matter movement Alicia Garza writes, "We perpetuate a level of White supremacist domination by reproducing a tired trope that we are all the same, rather than acknowledging that non-Black oppressed people in this country are both impacted by racism and domination, and simultaneously, BENEFIT from antiblack racism."[3] Acknowledging the differences in how we experience racism is central to cultivating solidarity. Empathy conjured up through an appeal to our supposed common oppression, on the other hand, runs the risk of erasing and diminishing the complexities of racialization that are distinct to different racial groups.

As we filed out of the town hall, I overheard Black students bemoan the unproductive, narcissistic White tears that distracted attention from Black students' testimonies. I grew anxious thinking about how they might lump Amy's outburst, and the rest of the Asian Americans by association, in with the theatrical displays of White guilt and fragility. While I didn't fully agree with Amy, I did in many ways understand her. Hearing the stories that Black Mills students shared helped me realize how displaced I actually felt at my PWI at times. Our experiences were not interchangeable, yet I was reminded of the undercurrent of exclusion I felt at Mills and institutions before this. In the centering of Black experiences at the town hall, I witnessed Amy gain language and take permission to unpack her own experiences of racial discrimination and exclusion. While she leaned into her own story to cultivate empathy and support for Black students at Mills, she also made inaccurate equivalencies. In so doing, she deflected energy away from the purpose of the town hall, which was to discuss the anti-Black hate statement, and the specificity of abuse and harassment Black students faced on our campus.

When there is so much collective pain among Black folks (that I had mostly been ignorant to and silent about), and I feel my own racialized pain suddenly reawakened and tugging at me, how do I actually show up to these moments and movements? In her seminal essay "Age, Race, Class, and Sex: Women Redefining Difference," Audre Lorde writes, "It is not our differences which separate women, but our reluctance to recognize those differences and to deal effectively with the distortions which have resulted from the ignoring and misnaming of those differences." Age, race, class, and sex differences, among other forms of identity, are wrought with power. Thus, acknowledging our differences in how we experience these identities enables us to see the challenges and dehumanization distinct to different groups, preparing us to see each other in our whole, nuanced, and actual complexities. Recognizing difference, rather than conflating our racialized experiences, is what mobilizes meaningful solidarity.

Amy clearly had painful experiences of racism she needed to unpack. While her timing and execution were off, the incident made me wonder, what *is* distinct about Asian Americans' experiences of racial discrimination and trauma, and when do we process it? Instead of a pent-up outburst of over-identification with Black experiences, what would healthier, more generative outlets look like for us to identify, grieve, and mobilize over our distinct experiences of racialization as Asian Americans? In order to build interracial solidarity in recognition of our shared, yet distinct, racial pain, we would also have to hear Amy's unique stories of racial victimization on campus. And while this town hall was clearly not the time or place, why hadn't we created or found any alternative times and places and spaces? These questions scrambled in my head as I wondered what it would look like to take Lorde's words seriously, and build shared power from our very different experiences of racism.

If Amy's impassioned speech was on one end of the spectrum of reactions to the Black Lives Matter movement (BLM), another end of the spectrum was indifference. I noticed silence, and what I perceived as apathy, among many of my East Asian friends in Asian ethnoburbs and churches in response to the shooting of Michael Brown and the subsequent protests. While posting on social media is not everything, I observed a deafening silence on my social media platforms from these friends about the racial uprising. While their silence may be tied to indifference, I also wondered if their disengagement sprung from complicated questions about belonging and exclusion.

In a study on Asian Americans' indifference to BLM, sociologist Aggie Yellow Horse and coauthors found a higher sense of belonging associated with lower odds of reporting indifference to the BLM movement.[4] In other words, those who felt like they belonged were less indifferent about anti-Black racism. Sociologists note that belonging is central to connecting individuals to social change,[5] and this is achieved by how one knows the social rules of engagement (e.g., the existence of a shared culture) and perceives the right to participate in the development of social rules (e.g., perceived decision-making power).[6] Chinese American author and activist Grace Lee Boggs wrote, "You cannot change any society unless you take responsibility for it; unless you see yourself as *belonging* to it and responsible for changing it" (emphasis added). Overall, regardless of nativity status, Asian Americans have the lowest sense of belonging compared to all other racialized groups, even compared to Latinos, who also have a large number of foreign-born group members. Lacking a sense of belonging may come from an internalized form of racist nativism, where Asian Americans feel estranged from decision-making and civic engagement processes in the US, thus cultivating a sense of indifference about US-based social movements like BLM.

In the same study, a sense of belonging was significantly higher for US-born Asian Americans compared to their foreign-born counterparts, who were 19 percent more likely to report indifference to BLM compared to US-born Asian Americans. This nativity difference is similar to other forms of political participation, where foreign-born Asian Americans are less likely to engage in both formal and informal political participation.[7] The assumption behind this finding is that the immigrant generation feels less civic belonging and does not understand anti-Black racism upon arrival, but their understanding of civic engagement and racism increases with more time in the US.[8] While Asian immigrants may have less understanding of race relations in the US context than their US-born counterparts, the authors of this study argue, "it is problematic and paternalistic to assume that Asian immigrants do not have racial consciousness until their arrival as it overlooks transnational and historical racial formations and anti-Black racism in Asia." Rather, scholars propose interrogating if Asian Americans' indifference is another form of performing Whiteness, derived from internalizing racism as an adaptive survival strategy, related to assimilation, to survive White supremacy.[9]

Staying uninvolved with racial and political issues may offer Asian Americans a perceived sense of protection as racial minorities in the US, especially considering how many of our families immigrated to quiet ethnoburbs from contexts where political dissent was punished with state-sanctioned brutality and violence. For many of our elders, martial law, Tiananmen Square, and other traumatic instances of political unrest and repression may loom insidiously in their collective memory. In creating our own safety through ethnoburbs, ethnic churches, and protected ethnic spaces, we erected racial boundaries that impeded connection and solidarity with other racial groups, especially Black Americans, and limited our ability to engage with historic racial uprisings. When I asked friends in the ethnoburb what they thought about BLM and the protests in Ferguson, many of them hadn't heard the news. The insularity of our protected ethnic spaces not only inhibited a shared politic of interracial solidarity but in some cases, precluded an awareness of racial injustice altogether.

In our ethnic spaces, where we centered our own communities and needs, we also rarely acknowledged our own racial pain. Our Asianness was normalized in the ethnoburb, so perhaps we didn't feel othered by it, or didn't have the language to name when we did experience racism. Until the rise in COVID-related attacks in 2020, I rarely heard my ethnoburb community talk about their experiences with race. They seemed disassociated.

Expanding on psychological definitions of dissociation, critic David Eng and psychotherapist Shinhee Han define racial dissociation among Asian Americans as "psychic mechanisms of self-protection in the face of overwhelming social stress and pressure." In *Racial Melancholia, Racial Dissociation: On the Social and Psychic Lives of Asian Americans*, Eng and Han find that new Asian immigrants in particular may feel "psychically and racially nowhere" in the Black/White racial landscape where they are simultaneously invisible and hypervisible, paradoxically racialized in a society that claims to be color-blind. Thus, racial dissociation functions as a coping mechanism to survive the cognitive dissonance, whereby Asian Americans preserve ourselves by disconnecting from emotionally charged mental conflicts and self-reflection that highlight these racial contradictions. "They didn't mean it that way," "I'm just being sensitive," or "We don't have it that bad" are common narratives I hear from Asian Americans after experiencing everything from a microaggression to explicit and violent, racialized mistreatment. Through racial dissociation, we gaslight ourselves out of our own racial victimization.

Contrastingly, BLM as a social movement is adamant about the centrality of race, insisting that White supremacist racial violence continues to affect Black daily life and material outcomes. BLM's message revealed the cracks in our color-blind, individualistic racial ideologies, and disturbed the ways we disengaged from larger racial tensions in this country through racial dissociation. BLM visibilized this country's racial contradictions, and their movement uncomfortably reminded us of our own vulnerability as racialized US subjects.

In my research on Chinese American evangelicals in 2021, respondents I interviewed often disapproved of White evangelicals' prejudicial attitudes toward Latino and Black Americans. However, they never mentioned White evangelicals' attitudes and treatment toward Chinese Americans or Asian Americans. They failed to connect former president Trump's racialized comments about COVID-19 to White evangelicals' support for him and his statements about China. Ultimately, my respondents didn't include themselves as a targeted racial group in their critique of White evangelicals. I found that while their Chinese ethnic church was a site to disassociate from Whiteness and racial tensions, it also reproduced the Black/White binary, whereby Asian Americans are neither privileged nor disadvantaged, but absent from the conversation about race completely. Lacking categories and discourse on how to situate themselves in racial justice movements, they expressed a sense of what I've coined "racial placelessness," taking themselves out of their own analyses on race and racism altogether.

Indifference to social movements matters because it is not value-neutral, nor is it an absence of opinion. It operates with racial disassociation and racial placelessness to make us complicit with White supremacy and oblivious to the racial struggles of not only Black Americans but our own. Indifference is an intentional choice to opt out of racial struggle, "to claim a solitude that can provide certain protections and freedoms afforded by privileges"[10] we have as non-Black people of color. But this indifference comes at the cost of our own racial consciousness and conviction. Similarly, silence—a manifestation of indifference—is its own form of anti-Black racism, which can even lead to violence as we consent to White supremacist ideologies, regardless of intentions. In other words, it is not necessarily enough for Asian Americans to "not be racist," but one must be racially conscious and "antiracist" in the system of White supremacy.[11]

I centered my ministry at this time around trying to be antiracist. Noticing an absence of outrage and engagement from my community, I frequently asked, "What's our place as Asian Americans in racial justice?" What's revealing about this question is that it assumes we don't have a place as Asian Americans in racial justice movements to begin with, as if we haven't already been victimized by and fighting racial injustice in the US for decades. My question reflected my own racial dissociation and longing: for permission, for legitimacy to speak on racial issues as an Asian American, and for clarity on my position in this country's racial politics.

IF AMY'S ENTHUSIASTIC OVERIDENTIFICATION WITH BLACK struggle is on one end of the spectrum and racially disassociated indifference is on another, still another reaction to racial injustice emerged from Asian Americans later that year, solidifying the ideological heterogeneity among our community in regard to race. In November 2014, just three months after the murder of Michael Brown in Ferguson, Akai Gurley, a twenty-eight-year-old unarmed Black man and father of a two-year-old, was walking down the stairs of his apartment building when a bullet ricocheted off a wall and pierced his heart. The gun was fired by Peter Liang, who was on patrol eighteen months after graduating the New York City Police Academy. As Gurley lay in his own blood, his friend tried to revive him as Liang passed by without helping. Liang became the first and one of the few police officers indicted in a police shooting case, and the jury found him guilty of manslaughter and official misconduct.

During Liang's trial, the media repeatedly presented Liang as the model minority, striving with his immigrant family and making his way as an inexperienced and harmless "rookie cop." Meanwhile, Gurley was criminalized as a "drug-dealing thug" with a criminal record. These racialized, stereotypical portrayals of Liang and Gurley incited racial conflicts, and the case mobilized Asian American activism rarely seen since the 1992 Los Angeles riots and the 1982 murder of Vincent Chin.[12] Because Liang was the first among the police officers indicted, and the other officers were White, enraged pro-Liang Asian Americans felt that Liang was scapegoated to assuage national attention from rising racial tensions that year. Rather than confront the anti-Black systemic racism highlighted by the unjust police killings of Black people that year, Asian American pro-Liang groups used racial victimology and anti-Blackness as discursive strategies to center racism against Chinese Americans. In their rallies, their dominant narrative was about the silencing of Asian American issues in the hypervisibility of Blackness in US politics, and a refusal to be the "silent Asians." In her essay "Complicity and Resistance: Asian American Body Politics in Black Lives Matter," Asian

American studies scholar Wen Liu explains that this discourse is aligned with the conservative opposition to BLM, where Chinese American protestors held ALL LIVES MATTER signs in pro-police rallies endorsing the White supremacist racial hierarchy that is built on Black criminality. Pro-Liang groups also employed American Dream discourse, where Liang's "unfair" indictment was framed as a hindrance for the racial uplift and progress of the model minority. Here, anti-Blackness is not just a prejudicial attitude against Black people but an adoption and performance of White supremacist racial ideologies about Black criminality, the American Dream, and Asian American merit.

The Liang case exposed an extreme of opinions within the increasingly diverse Asian American community, ideologically divided post-Ferguson. On the other side of pro-Liang, pro-police activism, the case reenergized a commitment among Asian Americans to stand in solidarity with other communities of color. Under #AsiansforBlackLives, Asian American activists drew on historical and contemporary Afro-Asian solidarity images of Asian American activists, like Yuri Kochiyama, Grace Lee Boggs, and Richard Aoki, protesting alongside Black Power activists against police violence. These images stressed the interdependent histories of Black and Asian communities, who built Afro-Asian solidarity toward the end of World War II on a transnational anti-imperialist politic, where national liberation movements in Africa and Asia against Euro-American colonialism inspired a vision of interracial solidarity among Asian and Black communities in the US. For Asian American BLM activists in 2016, historicizing Afro-Asian solidarity demonstrated that #AsiansforBlackLives is indeed "temporally legitimate and morally justifiable,"[13] bringing a sense of urgency to return Asian American pan-ethnicity back to its roots of interracial, internationalist solidarity. Further, in claiming solidarity with Blackness, Asian American activists sought to move beyond the awkward position of neither White nor Black, but to exist as a relevant and legitimate racial community with a stake in dismantling White supremacy.

The pro-police Chinese American communities and the #AsiansforBlackLives activists ran into direct conflict as the Liang case evolved. We witnessed an Asian America organizing for cross-racial solidarity, alongside an equally mobilized Asian America promulgating anti-Black racial agendas that would exempt Liang from accountability for killing Gurley. Asian American scholars argued that the intensified racial conflicts in the US, and the increasing heterogeneity of the Asian American community and its racial politics, ultimately reveal Asian Americans as flexible racial subjects that simultaneously claim and reject affiliation with the state and its institutions, like policing. As racial and political tensions continued to escalate, Asian Americanness became a perceivably contested and fragmented category, with different Asian American communities claiming their own positionality for and against BLM.

The diverse backgrounds, lived experiences, and identities that fall under the Asian American banner contribute to the complex racial positioning and divergent racial ideologies of our community, often on full display during historic moments and movements like BLM. Asian American positionality in the US challenges theories of racial stratification that traditionally focus on a Black/White binary, where Black people are situated at the bottom and White people at the top of the White supremacist racial structure. This framing largely ignores the nuances of racism that other racialized and minoritized people experience. To include growing numbers of Asian American and Latino demographics, Bonilla-Silva proposed a triracial stratification system, where Asian Americans are positioned in between White and Black people with three categorizations: "Whites," "honorary White" (e.g., East Asian Americans), and "collective [Black]" (e.g., darker-skinned and disadvantaged Southeast Asian Americans). Similar to Claire Jean Kim's racial triangulation theory, this conceptualization pushed the discourse on racial relations beyond the Black/White binary. However, scholars argue that these frameworks still inadequately explain the racialization of Asian Americans because they fail to capture the heterogeneous experiences *within* racialized and minoritized populations,[14] which contribute to the ideological extremes exemplified in Asian American responses to BLM and the Liang case.

Despite our heterogeneity, pan-ethnic organizing continues to be a common strategy to mobilize diverse Asian Americans for racial justice. At the height of BLM activism in 2016, and again in 2020, Asian American BLM allies wrote a set of letters to address anti-Blackness across generations in our own communities. The letters have been translated into more than twenty-three languages, and since adapted by Latino and other communities of color. The Letters for Black Lives project highlights the differential distribution of life chances under White supremacy, connecting the dots between criminalization, police, and Black death.[15] The popularity of the Letters project seemed to spike in 2016 and 2020, when momentum around BLM increased, but also after police killings that involved Asian American cops. Peter Liang in the murder of Akai Gurley in 2016, and Tou Thao's complicity in the murder of George Floyd in 2020, instigated questions and crises around identity, complicity, and solidarity among Asian Americans.

The letters centered the systemic nature of police violence against Black Americans, the specificity of anti-Black racism (and its differences from racism that Asian Americans have experienced), and the central role of White supremacy in dividing our communities. The project assumes that co-racial messengers can alter the racial attitudes of individuals, and that individuals are more open to persuasion from people who look like them and are in relationship with them. However, given that Asian Americans have relatively low levels of pan-ethnic group identity, and strong divisions persist among Asian Americans across national origin, linguistic, religious cultural lines,[16] Asian Americans may not actually be persuaded by these co-ethnic invitations in the same way as other minority groups in the US. In fact, a study by political scientists Maneesh Arora and Christopher Stout found that Asian Americans respond equally positively to co-ethnic and White messengers.[17] Given Asian Americans' lower levels of pan-ethnic group consciousness, the utility of co-ethnic mobilization under the Asian American banner remains in question.

And yet we continue to mobilize as Asian Americans to bring our families and communities along. Witnessing the significant roles of Peter Liang and Tou Thao in the racist police killings, the Letters project was a valiant, communal effort to confront our folks through transformative dialectics.

Through the Letters, we sought to show one another and the world that we take responsibility for our communities, and that anti-Black racism is both a structural and interpersonal issue, requiring difficult conversations and entire overhauls in institutions, as well as in our own homes. As a racial group often erased from conversations on race, we inserted our subjectivity in the movement for Black lives through the Letters project. Neither Black nor White, but something else, often slippery and forgotten altogether, we constructed ourselves out of racial placelessness through our own strategies for solidarity and collective liberation.

AS ANTI-ASIAN RACISM AND XENOPHOBIA SPIKED DURING the COVID-19 pandemic, many Asian Americans had to acknowledge that privileges, such as US-born status, US citizenship, educational attainment, and professional jobs, did not protect them from scapegoating, racism, and xenophobic hate incidents. Despite some Asian Americans' ambivalence to identify with the pan-ethnic collective because of the label's lack of specificity, Asian Americans were once again homogenized as targets of racial violence. When Trump tweeted, "China virus" in March of 2020, the broader public didn't care if you were first-generation Chinese American or third-generation Filipino American. Despite our growing numbers and diversity, COVID-19 forced us to confront the reality that we remain flattened, homogenous, and dehumanized under the White gaze.

The yellow peril stereotype reemerged at this time, eerily

similar to the 1900 plague when images of Chinese as diseased justified the scapegoating of and violence against Chinese immigrants. A case of a deceased Chinese man in San Francisco on March 6, 1900, caused hysteria, and city officials quarantined San Francisco Chinatown with ropes and barbed wire. Up to thirty-five thousand Chinese residents were kept inside densely populated and slum-like conditions without access to health care, while White residents were escorted out. Chinatown in Honolulu was set on fire during this time. Over a century later, COVID-19 served as an exogenous shock, uncovering, not creating, anti-Asian racism that had always been there.

Unprecedented to me, 2020 was the first time I witnessed the floodgates open to name the racism that Asian Americans face. Members of our community shared experiences of racial violence and discrimination on social media, with one another, and on campuses and workplaces through forums and town halls. Through pressure from Asian American activists and journalists, news media began to cover anti-Asian attacks, especially on our elders. We collectively grieved our ongoing racial status as outsiders to this country, loudly and publicly. This racial awakening was reminiscent of historic moments during the Asian American movement in the late-1960s to mid-1970s and in the aftermath of Vincent Chin's murder in 1982, when larger exogenous shocks uncovered systemic racism and inspired large numbers of Asian Americans to speak out and organize under the pan-ethnic banner. This racial consciousness-raising reminded me of Amy at Mills. I wondered how she, and we, would have benefited from these conversations earlier. If we had created this kind of space to acknowledge our own racialized pain, how would we have shown up differently, or at all, to other instances of racial injustice prior? Instead, many of us were asleep in racial dissociation.

In our grief, our responses to anti-Asian hate were often at odds with one another. One dominant narrative of anti-Asian violence that emerged in the wake of the pandemic was of an Asian American, often an elder or a woman, brutally attacked by a person who "appears to be Black." This narrative circulated through viral videos on social media. Regarding this Black-on-Asian trope, scholars Janelle Wong and Rossina Zamora Liu wrote,

> The media arc of anti-Asian violence—historically a symptom of White supremacy—quickly turned from the China-focused rhetoric of a White president and the heinous actions of White mass shooters to a focus on Black individuals physically assaulting Asian American elders. . . . The Black-on-Asian crime narrative has not only (re)ignited the Black-Asian conflict trope but seems to have also illuminated an undercurrent of anti-Blackness in narratives of Asian American victimization and perceptions of safety.

IN VOICING OUR GRIEVANCES ABOUT RACIAL VICTIMIZATION as Asian Americans, I witnessed the seduction of anti-Blackness within our community. As Wong and Liu argue, discourse around Black criminality became intertwined with Asian victimization. Further, right-wing politicians and media outlets strategically weaponized the Black-on-Asian crime narrative to redirect scrutiny away from the violent xenophobia of Donald Trump and White nationalists. Even more disturbing is how we subscribed to this narrative, often normalizing assumptions of Black criminality more quickly than we interrogated White supremacist leaders and mass shooters, deeming the latter as anomalies.

In both American and Asian media outlets like WeChat and Weibo, tropes of Black people as criminals acting violently toward Asian Americans circulated wildly. For many of us, our family members' perspectives were reinforced by personal experiences of discrimination, an underdeveloped understanding of systemic racism, and homogeneous social networks and social media bubbles, like WeChat.[18] Contrary to many of the images of Black criminality, the majority of perpetrators of anti-Asian hate incidents during the pandemic were disproportionately White, and Black individuals made up only a minority of offenders in anti-Asian incidents. In two separate studies, Wong[19] and historian Melissa Borja[20] found that three-quarters of offenders of anti-Asian hate crimes and incidents were White, and politicians who made anti-Asian statements and supported discriminatory policies and proposals were White, male, and affiliated with the Republican Party. Still, myths of Black-on-Asian violence insidiously permeated the media, policy responses, and our collective consciousness, motivating carceral responses reliant on increased policing.

I lived and worked in Oakland Chinatown for six years. At times, my apartment building and office were in the background of viral videos circulating of Asian elders getting attacked by Black individuals. At the height of these attacks, my parents called me to say, "We're so glad you don't live in Oakland anymore. It's too dangerous there." Implicit in their comment was the threat of Black criminality in urban areas like Oakland. And yet, Oakland was where I witnessed the most innovative, community-based strategies and movements of solidarity to keep Asian Americans safe. As many used anti-Asian attacks to call for more policing, with celebrities even offering exorbitant bounties on social media to catch perpetrators, reputable organizations with long-standing trust in the community like AAPI Women Lead and Asian Pacific Environmental Network, among others, were on the ground, addressing the root causes of violence, caring for victims of hate incidents, and keeping our communities safe. They organized those within and beyond the Asian American community to provide mutual aid to victims, safety escorts to elders, and local peace rallies and walks to provide a sense of security for merchants and neighbors. Oakland residents reported that their public safety hotline was more timely and responsive to victims of crime than the Oakland Police Department.

The Black Bay Area, an anti-gentrification group, fundraised to support Asian American organizations in Oakland and San Francisco, while groups like the Anti-Police Terror Project, the Ella Baker Center for Human Rights, and the Asian Pacific Environmental Network collaborated on initiatives to support Chinatown businesses, provide mutual aid to both Black and Asian communities in Oakland, and show solidarity. The grassroots nature of these efforts contrasted initiatives from the White House increasing police presence, creating task forces, and passing hate crime legislation. Recognizing that many communities of color, including Asian

Americans, do not feel safe or served by the police, these organizers confronted anti-Asian violence without relying on law enforcement institutions. The abolitionist slogan "We Keep Us Safe" circulated among these multiracial coalitions.

In the wake of the national reckoning on anti-Blackness and police brutality, transformative justice and abolitionist organizers created solutions centered on eliminating the root causes of violence, healing harm, and building community. They drew upon much of the Black-led abolitionist discourse, organizing, and leadership from the racial uprising the year prior. In a panel discussion titled "Reckoning with Anti-Asian Violence: Racial Grief, Visionary Organizing, and Educational Responsibility," Executive Director of National Asian Pacific American Women's Forum Sung Yeon Choimorrow emphasized, "I don't feel any safer with more law enforcement on the streets. It's a whack-a-mole approach. It's reactive and doesn't keep people safer." Instead, the community has been advocating "for a community unity awareness approach, so that we support and look out for each other."

In this same conversation, Asian American scholars also recognized the limitations of hate crime framing and legislation. Scholar Dr. Leigh Patel expanded, "[Hate crime] is not a robust enough term. It collapses into individualism and relies on a criminal justice system that is interested in increasing the militarization of the police force." In her public appearances, Dr. Connie Wun, founder of AAPI Women Lead, frequently rejected the use of violence against Asians, especially massage parlor workers, migrant workers, and sex workers to increase police surveillance and reify the carceral state. These grassroots, abolitionist organizers and scholars worked overtime to shift the mainstream narrative away from anti-Black criminality toward community-based solidarity, safety, and abolition.

BEING ASIAN IN THE US POSITIONS US AS BOTH MODEL MINORI-ties and perpetual outsiders, and we precariously exist both as exemplars and as the "Chinese virus." Liu writes that state and interpersonal violence against Asian Americans is actively erased in order to construct us as citizen-subjects benefiting from the myth of US multiculturalism. This obscures ongoing racial antagonism in the US, granting our country the cultural and moral "legitimacy" to continue dominating global neoliberal affairs in the Asia Pacific and the Global South, where racial violence manifests as ongoing imperialism and militarism. By erasing the racism Asian Americans experience domestically to promulgate the myth of American postracial multiculturalism, the US attempts to legitimate itself to intervene in geopolitics and perpetrate racial violence abroad.

As we have been invisible in US history, the violence of that erasure has rarely been acknowledged. In the aforementioned panel discussion, scholar Dr. Betina Hsieh shared, "Another facet of the pain that makes it more complicated is a lack of acknowledgment of our racialized trauma as Asian Americans, a lack of awareness of the history of anti-Asian violence in this country, and the invisibility and oversimplification of Asian Americans' experiences—experiences which are rich with resistance, coalition, and solidarity." Feeling reduced and overlooked has engulfed our racial consciousness, underpinning our racial attitudes. Whether we overidentify with Black struggle and practice people-of-color-blindness, use model minority racial logics to assert our own "deservedness," ground our own victimhood in messages of Black criminality, or dissociate altogether, our racial status as neither Black nor White, but invisible and racially placeless, is a wound that bleeds into our responses to racial injustice. To heal the wound, we must visibilize it, make room for its full affect. And to prevent future harm, we must internalize that, throughout history, we have always been safer and freer to become visible when we align with other communities of color, not with Whiteness. We keep each other safe.

The wound of feeling racially placeless and that our experiences with racism go unrecognized reopened for myself as I navigated the anti-Asian racism during the pandemic. As I made political education zines sharing my own racial grief, Black individuals from different parts of my life, women and queer folks in particular, emerged as allies to support me, uplift my voice, and process with me. They asked questions, shared their own thoughts, and cried with me. In 2021, I did three events with Black creators and educators who specifically invited me onto their platforms to address anti-Asian sentiment in Black communities. Eulanda, who hosts the Instagram travel page @dipyourtoesin, invited me to speak on an Instagram Live about the attacks, situating the events in the historical context of yellow peril and the racialization of Asians in the US. She conducted the interview with care, setting community guidelines with her followers, preparing a safety plan if the conversation got hijacked by trolls, and making space not just for my expertise but for my humanity. I felt not only seen but radically embraced in one of my most tender moments. And this is another way we heal from invisibility: to show up, to share, and to let others see and hold us.

Given our divergent experiences and politics, our ideologies about race and responses to racism are cacophonous. And yet, in our discordant responses, I posit there can be meaning and beauty in the clamor. Because for many of us, we are seeing and voicing ourselves for the first time. In the racket, we are certainly not silent. We are moving from racially nowhere to everywhere. We may be incongruous, but a cacophony, by definition, is audible. And our noise is evidence that we are coming out of invisibility, on our way to make music and purpose out of what it means to be Asian American. But not all noise is good noise; it is with urgency that we consistently lend our voices to tune the song of Asian America toward one of interracial solidarity and collective freedom, not of Black criminality and carcerality. We keep us safe.

speak

What is one way you can challenge yourself to show up, right here and right now?

I'm calling to urge our senator to support the ceasefire resolution. And since we're here ... to codify abortion rights, legalize marijuana, and protect trans kids.

Fears are valid, but can also be overcome. How can you work through your fears about using your voice so you don't end up silencing yourself?

Hi, are you accepting new patients? I'm looking to start therapy.

You will make mistakes and probably look stupid at some point. How will you repair harm and continue to show up?

I'm sorry. I didn't know. How can I make things right?

We can feel afraid, and we can still show up.

5

Ethnic Studies Helps Us Breathe Again

ETHNIC STUDIES HELPS US BREATHE AGAIN! was printed in large, bold black letters on mustard yellow paper and plastered onto a door with Scotch tape. It stood out among a constellation of colorful signs that read, ETHNIC STUDIES NOW!, KNOW HISTORY KNOW SELF, and DR. ALLYSON TINTIANGCO-CUBALES. It caught the corner of my eye as I walked down the first floor of the Ethnic Studies and Psychology building at San Francisco State University (SFSU). I counted the room numbers as I searched for the conference room where the Asian American Studies Master's Open House would be held. I reread the yellow sign. *That feels dramatic,* I thought to myself, hyperfocusing on the exclamation. *I breathe just fine,* as I side-eyed the sign and continued on my way. Despite my skepticism, my curiosity carried me onward toward the open house. As our country continued to brutally kill Black people and acquit their murderers, I longed for a more robust understanding of racial politics and my place in it, so I journeyed across the Bay Bridge from East Oakland to South San Francisco to see what this open house might yield me.

Little did I know, the campus I walked on held decades and legacies of student activism, rebellion, and revolution. SFSU's campus was the physical site where students practiced civil disobedience, faced police violence, and later that year, would starve themselves in a hunger strike to defend and advance the College of Ethnic Studies. I was not merely walking into an information session but crossing the threshold into a building that housed student activism and community imagination. In predominantly White institutions that prioritized White interests and demanded students of color to assimilate, Ethnic Studies was a safe space to breathe again, and to be unassimilable.

Historically, Ethnic Studies emerged from social movements in the 1960s. Inspired by the civil rights movement and decolonization movements throughout the Global South, the push for Ethnic Studies was grounded in the demand for collective liberation and self-determination. Students, educators, and community members pressured schools, school districts, and textbook companies to include histories and paradigms that focused on issues of race, culture, power, and identity.[1] In California, students of color organized the Third World Liberation Front (TWLF) coalition at the San Francisco State University and University of California, Berkeley, campuses to fight for inclusion, democracy, and self-determination for students and faculty of color as a step toward decolonizing education.

At SFSU, the TWLF was an interracial coalition following

the initiative of the Black Student Union. With the Latin American Student Organization, Asian American Political Alliance, Philippine American Collegiate Endeavor, and Native American Student Union, these affinity groups became the TWLF to demand and implement Ethnic Studies. Together, the formerly siloed groups of minority students became the politicized identity *students of color*, creating their own curricula and teaching one another their histories without waiting for institutional support or approval. While they were underrepresented in the university, they became powerful through their joint struggle. They carved out a space to help one another breathe and belong at a PWI. Contrasting the neoliberal zero-sum rhetoric in anti–affirmative action cases that divide communities of color under the myth of "meritocracy," the fight for Ethnic Studies is a visionary example of communities of color in higher education building power together in solidarity. The TWLF's five-month student strike, the longest student revolt in American history, resulted in the founding of the first Ethnic Studies department at SFSU in 1969. Ethnic Studies became institutionalized through collective student action and rebellion.

The TWLF and early Ethnic Studies activists were inspired by the work of Frantz Fanon on decolonization. A Francophone Afro-Caribbean psychologist, political philosopher, and Marxist, Fanon wrote about and participated in Algerian independence from France, describing decolonization as not only a physical (and violent) struggle but also an educational one. Decolonial movements freed territories *and* the colonized people's consciousness from the oppression and control of the colonizer.[2] Violent revolution was fundamentally an educational one, intervening and healing the ways colonialism imprisoned the mind. Ethnic Studies pedagogy grounded in decolonial struggle directly takes on the traumatic histories and legacies of colonialism on Indigenous and Third World peoples, systematically critiquing and healing these communities from colonial trauma, including the trauma of seeing oneself as academically incapable.[3]

As I walked into the open house, it was more casual than I expected. We sat in a circle and introduced ourselves, and I noticed all of the professors were Asian American women of different ethnicities, ages, phenotypes, and areas of study. As I expected from professors, they spoke with authority and conviction, especially about their research. Unexpectedly, there was an air of care and hospitality in the room. They hugged, they laughed, they fed us. The space felt spiritual, almost religious. I asked a current student, Greg, what his experience in the program was like, and he replied, "Here, your healing is tied to your research." I had never considered education as a conduit for healing, nor had I encountered such nurture in an educational space before. Until then, education was about individualistic achievements in PWI-WAAs. I wondered if Asian American Studies could be a space where I could learn to accept my own queerness, get brave enough to leave Inter-Varsity, and find my purpose as an Asian American woman, activist, and maybe even scholar. I began my application for the program that night.

At the open house, my own epistemological categories for "Asian American" and "professor" began to expand and overlap. My understanding of myself as the "model minority"—yet racially placeless—in education systems began to unravel as I

witnessed dynamic Asian American women professors leading conversations about race in the US, speaking passionately
about anti-imperialist movements, and radically welcoming
me to join the table they built. Schools and universities are
racialized organizations, which sociologist Victor Ray describes
as meso-level racial structures central to the contestation over
racial meaning, the social construction of race, and stability
and change in the racial order.[4] Organizations, especially
schools, are central to the "process by which racial categories
are created, inhabited, transformed, and destroyed,"[5] according to sociologists Michael Omi and Howard Winant on racial
formation theory. Through the faculty and students, Asian
American Studies became the site that decentered Whiteness
in my education and reconstructed not only my understanding
of Asian American identity and politics but my own individual
agency. It took the big age of twenty-five, walking through the
Ethnic Studies building, to see professors who looked like me
and, subsequently, to claim myself as a scholar for the first
time.

As a discipline, Ethnic Studies is subversive to schools as
racialized organizations because it destabilizes Whiteness as
a credential as it adamantly centers the experiences, cultures,
and histories of colonized, minoritized, non-White people. In
her book *Community as Rebellion: A Syllabus for Surviving Academia as a Woman of Color*, Ethnic Studies scholar-activist and
professor Lorgia García Peña argues that Ethnic Studies challenges dominant, Eurocentric definitions of knowledge, where
history, art, and literature are owned and produced by White
people, and everything and everyone else is subjugated, hidden, silenced, or portrayed as unnecessary, extracurricular, or

folkloric. Ethnic Studies fills the gaps left by the Eurocentric education system, and connects our individual and community experiences to historical and social events such as colonialism, wars, migrations, and social movements. By trusting and putting our own community members in positions of authority, Ethnic Studies as a discipline is a critical, anticolonial site of knowledge production, learning, and teaching that expands racial categories, contradicts the violence of PWIs, and serves as an intellectual and spiritual home for students of color. Asian American Studies scholar and professor Karen Umemoto asserts Ethnic Studies as the struggle to redefine education, which is inherently connected to the redefinition of American society.

IN MY SECOND SEMESTER IN THE ASIAN AMERICAN STUDIES program, rumors spread about significant cuts to our department funding. My peers panicked, but out of naiveté, I wasn't worried. I assumed our program would at the very least make sure we got our master's degrees, and funding would somehow reappear for future cohorts. It wasn't until I accidentally walked in on one of my professors crying in the bathroom before class when I realized this might be bigger than I anticipated. She was nontenured, which meant her job was precarious even before the potential funding cuts. She, among dozens of adjunct faculty, was at risk of losing her position because of the systematic defunding of Cal State Universities, disproportionately impacting humanities. With expansive possibilities for solidarity, community action, and healing, Ethnic Studies should be implemented everywhere. In reality, the freedom dreams of Ethnic Studies are constrained by the neoliberal limitations of academia, with contingent faculty like my professor bearing the cost.

SFSU's College of Ethnic Studies, which housed Asian American Studies, announced in 2016 that it was operating with close to a four-hundred-thousand-dollar deficit. Years prior, the California State University system faced severe budget cuts and made sweeping setbacks to colleges across disciplines, asking each college to cut 10 percent of its budget. The College of Ethnic Studies took a higher cut than was proportionate to the rest of the campus and never fully recovered, straining over the following years to cover the salaries of lecturers, tenured faculty, and the graduate program, among other costs. According to American Indian Studies department chair at the time Andrew Jolivette, "Around 50 percent of the coursework that the college provides, some of which are required courses for SFSU students, [may not be] available in the fall." Jolivette reported that the graduate program was also at risk of closing, and the lecturers that made up 40 percent of the college's staff were at risk of losing their jobs.[6]

In the spirit of the original TWLF, students from Africana Studies, Chicanx Studies, American Indian Studies, Asian American Studies, along with community members and alumni, organized and formed the 2016 TWLF to defend and advance the College of Ethnic Studies. Shannon Deloso, the incoming president of SFSU's Associated Students, was among the student organizers at the forefront of negotiations with administration. She highlighted the long-standing disconnect between students' needs and the administration's corporate, neoliberal agenda, which downsized liberal arts and corroded Ethnic Studies. Leading with clarity and courage, Deloso reminded the campus community, "The administration has not seen the value of our people's story, and most importantly has underestimated the power that the students and community have when we unite."[7] Student organizers presented the administration with a list of demands, and escalated their struggle when four undergraduate students went on a hunger strike for ten days. By the end of the strike, SFSU administration agreed to several of the demands, including adding two full-time tenure-track faculty appointments in Africana Studies, working toward departmental status for the Race and Resistance Studies program, and developing Pacific Islander Studies. Like in 1969, student organizing, civil disobedience, and interracial solidarity protected and advanced the unassimilable, radical possibilities of the College of Ethnic Studies.

SFSU wasn't alone in its budget problems, and many of the CSU system's Ethnic Studies programs and departments were under threat or had already been dismantled by this time.[8] In addition to defunding, the adjunct crisis impedes Ethnic Studies and communities of color in academia. Faculty of color are a disposable labor force who serve and support the growing population of first-generation students of color, and are often instrumental in supporting students organizing with and for Ethnic Studies. Yet they are rarely part of the fabric of the institution, seldom in positions that would ensure truer representation and systemic change. Peña writes, "Following the neoliberal trend that affects all industries across the globe, the modern university is more concerned with cost reduction and the amassing of its endowment than with the production of knowledge and the well-being of its students." To maintain this model, universities overwhelmingly depend on low-paid graduate students and temporary and part-time teaching staff such as adjunct professors to carry teaching loads. Only 21 percent of faculty are tenured with job security,[9] while the rest are in precarious positions semester to semester, vulnerable to low wages usually below the federal minimum and the poverty line.

In addition to institutional barriers built into the neoliberal structure of academia, Ethnic Studies is under attack by conservative backlash in the larger fight in our country over the very history, identity, and integrity of this nation. Not only Ethnic Studies but school boards, K–12 schools, books, and higher education more broadly, are politicized sites of conflict over the purpose of education, what schools are allowed to teach, and, ultimately, who we are as Americans. As evidenced by recent controversies over banning books and critical race theory, different forms of conservative collective action have emerged to protect White supremacy. From desegregation to DEI, education continues to be a site to contest racial meanings and the very identity and roots of the US, and Ethnic Studies has long been one of its many battlegrounds.

Arizona's statewide ban on Ethnic Studies in 2010, in response to the Mexican American Studies program in Tucson Unified School District, was one of the most high-profile and reactive instances of opposition to Ethnic Studies. Additionally, in 2018, White parents in Central California mobilized to voice their discontent about the inclusion of Ethnic Studies as part of the state's graduation requirements, positioning White, Christian, American boys as victims of Ethnic Studies. In his article "Curricular Countermovements: How White Parents Mounted a Popular Challenge to Ethnic Studies," Ethan Chang conceptualizes these efforts as *curricular countermovements*: oppositional movements aimed to delegitimize programs that cultivate academic achievement and critical consciousness of youth of color. Across red and blue states, rural and urban communities, curricular countermovements are growing and thwarting the liberatory possibilities of Ethnic Studies.

More recently in 2021, the Texas State Board of Education (SBOE) initiated a review of the Texas Essential Knowledge and Skills (TEKS). Working groups of educators and experts drafted revisions to social studies and history courses and proposed Asian American and American Indian Studies elective courses in high schools across Texas. This was an imperfect, but significant step toward more inclusive curricula. On two occasions, I made the two-hour drive from Houston to the state capitol in Austin to join youth, educators, and community organizers to voice our support for the revisions and urge the board to implement the statewide Ethnic Studies electives.

As I sat with my colleagues in the SBOE meeting awaiting my turn to testify, the overwhelming numbers and energy of those who came to oppose Ethnic Studies and the social studies curricula revisions became suffocating. Under the fluorescent lights in the drafty room with the air-conditioning turned up way too high, we sat in rows, facing our state board members. In between us stood the podium for testimonials, alone in the center resembling a fighting ring. All of us who'd made the trek from Houston, Dallas, San Antonio, and other parts of the state were called up one by one to make our case in support of, or opposition to, the curricula changes in under two minutes. Texas flags were planted in every corner of the room, accompanied by armed security guards. Among the rows of testifiers, the sides we took were explicit and polarizing. Middle-aged White parents, mostly women, dressed in red, white, and blue, donned pins that read, DEFEND AMERICA. Visually, they had a strong collective identity. They strategically sat together, synchronously coughing, whispering, and shuffling on cue to create a flurry of disruption when they heard testimonies they disagreed with. At times, their noise escalated into loud and boisterous booing, taking time and attention away from the meeting as a board member would have to remind the room to follow decorum. They were strategically distracting and incredibly organized.

Their testimonials included themes commonly seen in the curricular countermovement against Ethnic Studies, including narratives of White victimhood (particularly for White boys), neoliberal logics that emphasize the economic purposes of schooling, and Christian patriotism. At the SBOE meeting, White moms, usually in tears, emphatically argued that the proposed revisions to the social studies curriculum were dangerous, devaluing of American exceptionalism, and facilitated by liberal indoctrination. They screamed about their children suffering emotionally from curricula (which had not been taught yet) that centered non-White histories and experiences, insisting these lessons were "not age-appropriate." The nationwide hysteria and misinformation over critical race theory exacerbated the debate, with much of the daylong meetings spent distinguishing CRT* from Ethnic Studies and the curricula changes.[10] Ultimately, capitulating to conservative backlash and opposition, the SBOE voted to postpone the process that they themselves initiated until 2025, and essentially reverse course on the progressive revisions.

Controversies over Ethnic Studies are tied to this country's contested collective memory and commitment to historical amnesia. In Texas, Asian Americans have been in the state as early as the late 1800s. Chinese contract laborers were the first Asian immigrants in Texas, recruited to work on the railroads in 1870 and again in 1881. Chinese immigration ceased for nearly sixty years with the passage of the Chinese Exclusion Act in 1882, but there was an exception in 1917 when General Pershing brought 427 Chinese refugees from Mexico to fight against Mexican revolutionary Francisco "Pancho" Villa.[11] These refugees were granted asylum to support US invasion into Mexican territory. The Asian American Studies elective

---

*   The politicization of and misinformation over CRT does the movement for Ethnic Studies a disservice, as Ethnic Studies built upon the theoretical framework of CRT to support a racial analysis of school inequities. CRT offers concrete tools for framing pedagogies of race, such as counterstorytelling and testimony, which, rather than adding the perspective of communities of color to a Eurocentric story, centralizes the experiences and narratives of people of color, thus legitimizing them as evidence to challenge and reframe dominant narratives about race, culture, language, and citizenship. For elected officials and advocates to work overtime distinguishing between Ethnic Studies and CRT in an effort not to polarize community members ultimately waters down the pedagogical purpose of Ethnic Studies to multiculturalism, defusing the critical, antiracist origins of Ethnic Studies. (Tintiangco-Cubales, et al. "Toward an Ethnic Studies Pedagogy" *The Urban Review* 47 (2015): 104–25.)

course included this lesser known, localized Asian Texan history. And yet, the SBOE voted against including the history of the Pershing Chinese in the eighth-grade social studies curriculum in their 2022 vote. As the South diversifies demographically and becomes increasingly non-White, White conservatives fight to preserve White supremacist legacies in the collective memory, from classroom curricula to Confederate monuments.

The staunch opposition to Ethnic Studies reveals its power to challenge racial meanings and power structures. The movement for Ethnic Studies destabilizes Whiteness by centering communities of color and combating historical amnesia. In line with Brazilian educator and philosopher Paulo Freire's critical pedagogical approach *conscientization* in *Pedagogy of the Oppressed*, Ethnic Studies equips oppressed communities to understand *and* act on the root causes of their oppression. Meanwhile, conservative curricula countermovements labor to protect and expand Whiteness in education by claiming Ethnic Studies is "anti-American" and "anti-White." These movements attempt to undermine not only Ethnic Studies but the progressive social movements Ethnic Studies teaches about and inspires.

ETHNIC STUDIES IS THREATENING NOT JUST BECAUSE IT CHALlenges White dominance in schools but because of its capacity for collective healing, within and beyond the classroom. Ethnic Studies gives language and tools to confront and transform realities of racial violence through revolutionary vision and care, bridging the divide between the ivory tower and community activism. The first time I heard the late historian Dr. Dawn Mabalon speak, she whispered, "History is the tsismis of the ancestors," with a smirk, as if letting us in on a secret. We were a classroom of fifty undergraduate and graduate Asian American volunteer student teachers in a Pin@y Educational Partnerships (PEP) training, a SFSU-based program preparing us to teach Filipino American Studies at local elementary, middle, and high schools across San Francisco. Founded in 2001 by Dr. Allyson Tintiangco-Cubales (known in the community as Ate Allyson) and her SFSU students, PEP was originally a lunchtime mentoring program at Balboa High School in the Excelsior neighborhood of San Francisco, which saw high rates of Filipinx dropout, teenage pregnancy, substance abuse, gang violence, and mental health issues. The lunchtime mentoring program evolved into PEP, a yearlong Filipinx American Studies class at Balboa. PEP produced critical educators and curricula at all levels of education and in the community, uniquely implementing transformative decolonizing classes and pedagogy that impacted students, as well as their families and neighborhoods.

Dr. Mabalon, award-winning scholar, activist, and professor at SFSU's history department (also Ate Allyson's bestie) often spoke at our PEP meetings. When she described the study and teaching of history as the tsismis, or gossip, of the ancestors, something unlocked in me. In one simple line, she inserted us as subjects of history, an academic discipline in an institution and in a country that regularly reduced us to objects. She used history to reconnect us to our ancestors, who have always held the indigenous wisdom and technology to survive White supremacist, colonial violence. While Asians in the US are often invisible, or at best relegated to one paragraph of a US history book, Dr. Mabalon's culturally-specific proclamation reframed and centered history around us and who we come from. Interrupting historical amnesia, she guided us from racial placelessness back into our intergenerational diasporic stories of survival and resistance. While I'm not Filipina, I owe much of my own conscientization to the critical pedagogy and community PEP welcomed me into.

As I got pushed out of InterVarsity, Ethnic Studies was my place to land, and my teaching barangay of other PEP teachers became like my church. We met every Wednesday night and taught every Friday morning together. We ended each meeting and class with the Unity Clap, increasing in volume, speed, and ferocity, culminating in the proclamation, "ISANG BAGSAK!," which translates into "one down" and signified "to fall and rise together." It was a ritual adopted from anti–martial law activists in the Philippines and the Filipino and Latino Farmworkers movement in Central California. In my longing for a political community and spiritual home, my Filipinx co-teachers and our rituals became a balm to former experiences in PWIs and Christianity, where I often felt spiritually isolated and racially nowhere.

The weekend before each semester, PEP held an over-night retreat. We shared our talam buhay, responding to the prompts: "Where are you from? Where are you now? Where are you going?" Teachers shared photographs, stories, and songs about their histories and hopes for the future. I shared about coming out of a traumatic season in InterVarsity, under-standing myself to be queer, facing rejection, and losing my religious community. Many of my co-teachers were also queer, and nearly all my co-teachers experienced some kind of religious baggage or trauma. In the opportunity to narrate my journey, my barangay's empathy and solidarity validated my pain. The weekend of connecting, training, and preparing for the school year felt like church camps I used to attend. The PEP community and its pedagogies became my healing.

All this feelings stuff wasn't just for its own sake. The talam buhay, the retreat, the intentional acts of community building centered around the concept that we as teachers needed to do deep identity work and healing in order to engage our students in an Ethnic Studies classroom. Research finds that effective K–12 Ethnic Studies teachers are aware of how their racial identity informs their teaching in their use of culturally and community responsive pedagogy.[12] While there are strong White and non-White Ethnic Studies teachers, being a person of color is a distinct asset. Regardless of race, however, the effectiveness of Ethnic Studies teachers hinged on their continuous reflection about their own identities, their relationships with the focal ethnic communities, and the impact of a Eurocentric system on their perspectives and sense of self.[13] By unpacking our own experiences of racialization, exclusion, and resilience as people of color in the American education system, we were better equipped to teach and connect with students of different identities at our school sites.

Through PEP, I witnessed what it could look like to be part of a neoliberal institution that threatened to defund Ethnic Studies, while still carving out radical, unassimilable, and imaginative spaces for communities of color to see and care for each other. Beyond PEP, this pedagogy of care was commonplace in my Asian American Studies graduate coursework. In an Asian American Health Issues class, professor Dr. Grace Yoo started every class with an extended check-in. These check-ins would often become very vulnerable spaces, with students sharing about mental health challenges and family or academic struggles. While this emphasis on care has led critics to argue that Ethnic Studies is not academically rigorous, my professors knew that mental health and overall well-being were prerequisites to critical learning. "Students don't care what you know until they know that you care," Ate Allyson often reminded us.

In their essay "Care Work: The Invisible Labor of Asian American Women in Academia," San Francisco State University professors Wei Ming Dariotis and Grace Yoo explain that care work performed by Asian American women in the academy, which I witnessed from Ate Allyson, Dr. Mabalon, Dr. Yoo, professor and student services director Dr. Daus-Magbual, and so many others, is a form of labor that involves intentional caring that allows students to feel seen and safe. This care work is labor that supports the emotional well-being and academic goals of students and colleagues, as well as the university itself. Ate Allyson describes Alagaan pedagogy (pedagogy of care) as central to her teaching: "I see that as teachers we have a responsibility to care as a central part of our work of teaching our students how to learn."[14] In a department where most students are minoritized, first-generation, often with plenty of financial and familial responsibilities, I witnessed our professors' care support our learning and facilitate our healing.

Pedagogies of care and decolonizing curriculum in Ethnic

Studies have profound impacts on student outcomes. Research shows that Ethnic Studies curriculum that reflects the experiences of students of color has a positive impact on student academic engagement, achievement, empowerment, empathy, attendance, literacy proficiency, graduation rates, and college enrollment, especially when linked with culturally responsive teaching grounded in high academic expectations. These outcomes persist regardless of the race of the student.[15] The Social Justice Education Project (SJEP) in Tucson, Arizona, is one of the best-documented cases of how education that decolonizes and teaches students to challenge racial oppression has positive impacts on students of color academically. Evaluations of SJEP's Chicana/o Studies over several years found that students enrolled in its courses graduated and went on to college at higher rates than other students in the same schools, and tested higher on the state's tests for reading, writing, and math.[16]

I dreamt about these expansive possibilities as I prepared to solo teach my first Ethnic Studies course at City College of San Francisco. As I created my syllabus for "Asian American History," I imagined talambuhays, healing circles, young minds in awe as we read Ronald Takaki's *Strangers from a Different Shore*, cohorts excelling academically and going on to become community organizers, and, of course, my students admiring my professor outfits. As the semester started, I learned that most of my students were newcomer Asian immigrants. Some were not fully proficient in English and not planning to stay in the US. Many took the course because it covered a general education requirement and had little interest in Asian American history. Several students were also parents, working full-time, or had other caretaking and financial responsibilities. In a city with an increasingly exorbitant cost of living, most of my students were just trying to get by. And then there were the handful of White male students who enrolled because they loved anime. My students texted, fell asleep, and worked on other coursework during my class. Romancing them to care about early Asian immigration histories and the tsismis of our ancestors was more challenging than I anticipated.

We spent one unit of the course examining the violent legacy of US imperialism in Hawai'i. As we read texts about early Asian migrant laborers recruited to work on sugar plantations in Hawai'i, eventually building pan-ethnic solidarity and immigrant communities on the islands, I wanted to make sure we were also aware of the Indigenous people who cared for the land before the plantations. We read, watched documentaries, and learned from native Hawai'ian speakers about the illegal overthrow of the Hawai'ian monarchy by the US government and plantation owners, the ongoing illegal occupation of Hawai'i, and the continual fight for Hawai'ian sovereignty today. These voices helped us challenge mainstream settler colonial narratives on Asian immigration that often erase Indigenous peoples and histories. I wasn't sure how much my students absorbed.

In their final paper, one student wrote about the connections between Native Hawai'ian and Aboriginal Taiwanese sovereignty movements. He had only been in the US for a few months, and shared how the systematic eradication of his own aboriginal culture and identity in Taiwan helped him understand and grieve the erasure of Native Hawai'ian culture and people at the hands of the American empire and corporate interests. His paper and in-class presentation examined both sovereignty movements, and he stressed the imperative to uplift Indigenous peoples' movements and embrace his own Indigenous lineage. This student named his own community's colonial wounds as he began to make connections toward anti-imperialist solidarity with Native Hawai'ians.

The news cycle under the Trump administration also gave no shortage of examples of the relevance of Asian American history. On the week we discussed early Chinese immigration and Chinese resistance in the courts to the exclusion laws, the Deferred Action for Childhood Arrivals (DACA) program was again under threat. On my drive to class, I made a game-time decision to alter my lesson plan for the day and devote the latter half of class to discussing DACA and inviting students to call their Congress members to share what DACA meant to them and their communities. Nearly all of my students were children of immigrants or immigrants themselves, and none of them had done advocacy calls to elected officials before. Together, we looked up our representatives, wrote a script as a class, and sent emails and made calls. Several of my students opted out because they did not feel comfortable exposing themselves with their own precarious immigration status, which I was sensitive to and in support of. These students participated by helping us draft the script and emails. I encouraged students to assess their own levels of risk and make decisions that would be best for them. I trusted them.

As I picked up my phone to call my own Congress member, I found myself suddenly feeling nervous. Because phone calls made me nervous, because the weight of what we were doing felt heavy, and because despite me leading this activity, I had never called my own elected officials before. But I looked around and saw my students of different ages, English language proficiencies, and backgrounds all doing it with me. I witnessed our classroom become what bell hooks calls "a site of possibility" that interrupted historical amnesia and cultivated community and solidarity. Through collective action, my students and I shared our own immigration stories and advocated for the protection of DACA recipients. While we didn't have the power to change laws, we created an ecosystem that cared for our undocumented community members, empowered one another to use our voices in new and uncomfortable ways, and facilitated individual and collective healing. Through Ethnic Studies, critical curriculum and pedagogies of care in my classroom worked to alchemize racial grief during Trump's presidency into critical understanding, reflection, and action.

The capacity for Ethnic Studies to confront and heal racial grief became even more apparent during the pandemic. Throughout COVID-19, communities of color were at greater risk of contracting the virus. Asian American children missed school not only because of stay-at-home orders but because they were afraid of racially motivated harassment and bullying. Students at SFSU reported experiencing fatigue because of the constant access that social media provided for news on the pandemic, anti-Asian racism, and anti-Black violence. Twenty percent of SFSU students also experienced race-related discrimination during the pandemic. Students felt sad, angry, overwhelmed, and fearful for their safety and the safety of their family members. Dr. Arlene Daus-Magbual, director of AANAPISI at SFSU, found "a need to hold space for our community in times of grief, anger, and sadness."[17]

With community organizations, other scholars, and students in the SFSU community, Daus-Magbual codeveloped and facilitated events, forums, and town halls in the wake of the murder of George Floyd, the Atlanta shooting, and rising racial tensions throughout the pandemic. These events served as onramps toward empathy, hope, and healing. Their event "Tatlong Bagsak for Black Lives: Combating Anti-Blackness in the Filipina/x/o Community," for example, provided space to discuss how Filipina/x/o American freedom is tied to Black liberation, how to be in solidarity for Black lives, and how to continue this critical dialogue around racial injustice. The event drew more than one thousand participants nationwide.

At the intersection of anti-Blackness within the Asian American community and anti-Asian violence running rampant throughout the US, Ethnic Studies as a site of care served as an antidote. Dr. Tintiangco-Cubales discussed the necessity of kinship during this time of racial grief: "When we think about reckoning with anti-Asian violence, we need to allow space for racial grief—for your grief and that of those whom you are in solidarity with. Not just solidarity, but kinship. We are kin with each other. . . . Racial grief isn't going away unless White supremacy goes away, unless racism goes away."[18] Dr. Russell Jeung, SFSU Ethnic Studies professor and cofounder of the Stop AAPI Hate campaign, similarly called for the community to move toward collective healing: "Drawing attention to our experiences by centering on our pain and grieving by connecting with each other and sharing these stories, that's how we get healed from racial trauma. This is our moment where we can take the pain and turn it around to offer hope."[19] Throughout the pandemic, Ethnic Studies provided a dialogical space, a sense of belonging, and an acknowledgment of grief. Following the legacy of TWLF, Ethnic Studies in this historical time of crisis moved our communities toward healing, solidarity, and activism.

EDUCATION IS SIMULTANEOUSLY A LIBERATORY AND COLO-nizing site.[20] Cultural anthropologist Alicia Chavira-Prado writes, "On one hand, [academia] represents liberation for the historically oppressed because its cornerstone, education, equips us to question critically, thereby enabling our decolonizing process." At the same time, academia is a racializing, colonizing institution in the politics of domination: "It ensnarls us into another form of colonization as it attempts to impose its own language, norms, expectations, and prescriptions, all of which form an academic culture that enshrouds theory and method."[21]

When I began applying to PhD programs, my motivation was community. With bell hooks's writings on pedagogy inscribed on my heart (and vision board), I longed for the institutional validation and letters behind my name to create classrooms that served as freedom spaces for collective liberation. I memorized my GRE vocabulary cards with a stack of books by Audre Lorde, Helen Zia, and Paulo Freire next to me. Like these scholar activists who came before me, I wanted the training and credibility to "write ourselves into history." A doctorate was the highest academic and professional ambition I had strived for in my life, and I felt anxiously inadequate as a first-generation college student.

While community was my initial purpose, I quickly found

myself romanced by the elitism of academia. The love bombing began when I received my first invitation for an in-person interview. They flew me out, put me up in a luxury suite in a five-star hotel, and wined and dined me in their handsome, centuries-old buildings (built by enslaved Africans). Meanwhile, academics I had read and cited for years wooed me, expressing interest in my research ideas and whispering sweet nothings in my ear about my intellect and talent. I had truly never had my ego stroked like this before. It was intoxicating. I drunkenly wondered, "Is this how White men feel all the time?" By claiming to desire and fight for me, these departments preyed on and soothed my impostor syndrome.

For a brief time, I found myself seduced and enchanted. Life as an academic in the ivory tower felt utopian. Spending my days reading and writing, sharing research with the "best" in our fields (as defined by them), pontificating to students about theory, I started striving to secure this life for myself. I struggled for publications, awards, and grants; I mastered their "canon" of dead White men whose work held little relevance to my community; and I found myself speaking more and more of statistics and theory and less and less of solidarity and liberation. While these concepts are not mutually exclusive, I noticed weird looks or silence when I mentioned community or radical politics. I convinced myself I was assimilating so that one day I could have the security to teach and do research on my own terms. But beneath the surface, I also wanted approval from an institution that I would never truly be enough for, and that would never truly be enough for me.

In *The Wretched of the Earth*, Frantz Fanon asserts assimilation as the first and foundational stage of the colonized intellectual, through which she adopts the values, paradigms, and interests of the colonizer. She becomes preoccupied with Eurocentric values like individualism and objectivity, even though nothing about her experience in the academy is objective. She is enticed to succeed in the colonial system and fill its senior positions, from administrators to experts to advisors. These positions fill her with a sense of stability, purpose, and superiority over her kin. In her arrogance, she is convinced that violent, disruptive methods of protest by the masses are ineffective and divisive. She fights for the colonizer and colonized to live in "peace," refusing to see the enduring power differential that exists between them, which can only be confronted through revolutionary, disruptive action. She works to translate the colonized for the colonizer. However, her insights are not driven by the people's realities, but by the colonizer's frameworks. Ultimately, the colonized intellectual aids and abets the colonizer. Fanon describes one of the many reasons why representation in colonial institutions does not necessarily beget material change.

And yet, the colonized intellectual can be liberated and part of liberation, as long as she aligns with the oppressed masses and merges her self-interest with that of the people. Fanon writes that this stage is "characterized by an understanding of what must be done for their people, causing their work to take on a more revolutionary form in attempts to inspire their citizens."[22] By putting to death the hyperindividualism of intellectualism and immersing herself among revolutionary social movements, the colonized intellectual can join the larger community to challenge oppressive institutions like academia. The nature of her intellectual work begins to transform and become revolutionary as she aligns with and is moved by the masses.

Education can liberate and colonize, and the colonized intellectual has the potential to dismantle the status quo as much as she can reify it. As long as I am in academia, it is imperative that I resist the colonization of my own consciousness at all costs. Assimilation into White institutions can feel insidiously compulsory. Seduced by the prestige, I was starved to beat their game so I could earn the credentials and never question my belonging again. And yet, running myself to the ground working to assimilate into their definitions of excellence would never be enough. No plethora of publications and awards would satisfy, because the extractive academic system depends on my feeling excluded to keep me overworking and contorting myself for them. The neoliberal academic institution thrives off my labor, compliance, and self-conscious surrender.

On the other hand, Ethnic Studies makes it possible to not only create unassimilable, radical spaces of community and healing but to become unassimilable and radical myself. Ethnic Studies is the container where I am affirmed in my belonging as a scholar, and am reminded that my security comes from merging my fate with that of the community, not with the institution. Ethnic Studies helps me breathe again, so that I may strive to become an intellectual for liberation, taking the resources and privileges of academia and composting them to serve revolutionary movements within and beyond the academy. In institutions that actively work to seduce, assimilate, and erase us, I return to this purpose frequently. Rather than fighting to belong to the university, I survive by rebelling against it, by making noise with my community at board meetings, and by building curricula and classrooms that cultivate freedom and solidarity. Lest I succumb to aiding and abetting this country's amnesiac commitment to Whiteness, I remain an unassimilable academic.

6

Revolutionary Spirituality

My connection to the tight-knit Asian American community in InterVarsity officially severed with their twenty-page internal position paper on human sexuality, published March 2015, stating, "Scripture is very clear that God's intention for sexual expression is to be between a husband and wife in marriage. Every other sexual practice is outside of God's plan and therefore is a distortion of God's loving design for humanity." With more than 1,300 employees on 667 campuses around the country at the time, InterVarsity gave us eighteen months to study the paper and nine video curriculum modules on InterVarsity's position. The curriculum did not engage any LGBTQ+-affirming voices, and relied heavily on the work of one popular conservative theologian, Wesley Hill, along with stories of staff and one transgender student. Nearly all of the individuals in the videos were White, while the main figureheads of the policy rollout were Asian American men, including their incoming president Tom Lin and current vice president Greg Jao.

The letter stated that InterVarsity employees are expected to both "believe and behave" in accordance with InterVarsity's theological position holding that any sexual activity outside of a husband and wife is immoral. For those who do not align, they are encouraged to "exercise integrity and come forward to resign within two weeks of revealing disbelief," and InterVarsity would start its process for "involuntary termination," concluding employment within a two-week period. LGBTQ+ individuals could remain on staff if they committed to celibacy and affirmed the position paper. The organization made a theological purge.

As I interrogated InterVarsity's homophobic theological position and policy—and my own place in the organization as a closeted, bisexual queer woman—one of my mentors, also a bisexual Asian American woman, warned, "I can't protect you if you can't comply with the doctrinal statement." Despite our shared identity, she aligned with the organization over her staff. As the policy rollout escalated, so did my verbal disapproval and resistance. During Urbana that year, InterVarsity's largest international conference, drawing thousands of attendees, I tweeted my disappointment over a plenary speaker's homophobic jokes made from the main stage. Later that day, the organization's supervisors cornered and berated me for "making the organization look bad." One supervisor tried to bully me into deleting my tweets, insisting that I "probably wouldn't feel comfortable with myself" if I left the tweets up. One of my Asian American mentors was called in

and witnessed the entire interaction in silence. Of the abandonment I felt from my spiritual community, the sharpest
betrayal came from the inaction of fellow Asian Americans.

As InterVarsity enforced their theological policy, it became
apparent that their leadership saw us—queer staff, students,
and allies—as disposable. As I now know, any employer that
calls its employees "family" should sound alarms, but at the
time, InterVarsity was my home and social network. Several
of us formed the InterVarsity queer collective to organize staff,
students, and alumni to protest the policy, write letters, and
push for dialogue with leadership about the policy rollout. In
response, InterVarsity used manipulative spiritual language,
like "grace" and "family," to instill fear and shame among those
who challenged them. When I questioned the homophobic,
White-centered curriculum presented by leadership, I was told
to be more "forgiving, gracious, and patient" with the process.
The heart palpitations and nausea in my body told me this was
violent, but the weaponization of spirituality silenced my own
intuitive wisdom.

I came to believe that the only way forward was to try to
change the organization from within, to continue to put myself in harm's way, and to overexpose myself to toxic leaders. I
swallowed the lie that I had to stay in this abusive relationship
with my employer and to be a martyr for the cause. Hitting
wall after wall, the queer collective and I decided to escalate
our movement publicly by speaking to Elizabeth Dias, *TIME*
magazine reporter, who ran an exposé. I was one of several
queer staff who came out as InterVarsity's whistleblowers.
A handful of our colleagues were supportive and prepared
to struggle with us, but the vast majority was silent. Several

InterVarsity staff flooded my direct messages and email inbox for bringing this shameful whirlwind on our "family."

Ultimately, nothing materially changed. InterVarsity implemented their theological position, and staff members were fired, or "involuntarily terminated." An unquantifiable number of us were gaslit, traumatized, and ultimately excommunicated for fighting for queer inclusion. Our exit seemed to be no loss to them at all, despite many of us having given years and decades to build this organization. After the article was published in *TIME*, my pastor at my Chinese home church, FCBC, made a sudden announcement the following Sunday service clarifying that the church did not align with my views stated in the article about InterVarsity. Up until then, FCBC was my source of spiritual, social, and financial support for my ministry with InterVarsity. After my pastor's announcement, the rest of my extensive church network fell out of my life.

"There is a particular abandonment of living outside of the blessing and belonging of our spiritual communities, especially for Asian Americans," shared Liz Lin, founder of Progressive Asian American Christians. "For Asian Americans who have to leave these protected ethnic spaces, there are not many options. You can go to a mainline queer-affirming church, but you'll likely be the only person of color there. With ethnic churches as community centers, tied to identity, family, and immigration stories, the decision to leave is latent with so much more than just leaving a faith tradition. It can feel like there are no places to land." Losing my InterVarsity community, and eventually my immigrant church, became one of the most devastating costs of refusing to assimilate into their heterosexism.

My experience with InterVarsity reveals how disposability politics permeates our sacred, spiritual spaces. Yu-Shuan Tarango-Sho, founder of Sacred Roots, explains, "The politics of disposability is a manifestation of White supremacy and capitalism, in that it's everywhere," including the spaces we labor to make our own. It's unsurprising, yet disappointing, that it was my own Asian American mentors who were the ones to carry out much of the violent policy implementation. With InterVarsity's expectation for us to "believe and behave" in accordance with their theological position, Reverend Dr. Ken Fong, former board of trustees member and outspoken pastor for LGBTQ+ affirmation in the church, described the process as "policing the mind." Instead of seeing everyone as inherently valuable and making room for difference, InterVarsity purged anybody who fell outside of their theological and ideological boundaries.

As I moved on from InterVarsity and divorced myself from evangelical spaces, I found myself internalizing its politics of disposability. As I sought to learn from more radical community organizers, I became my own version of an ideological purist. In my social services job after InterVarsity, I looked down on coworkers who worked with state institutions and "did not critique the system enough." I held a high bar for who I would engage with, and wrote off all the Bay Area tech industry Asians and Christian Asians who I perceived as apolitical and lukewarm. At the root of this pretension was fear and self-defense; I was protecting myself after the traumatic excommunication from InterVarsity. I needed to know who I was safe with. I could not imagine collaborating, or even engaging, across ideological differences, as I was still reeling from betrayal and mistrust from my overlapping spiritual and racial/ethnic communities. This also meant I often felt lonely and guarded in my hypervigilance.

In building community across ideological differences, I often question where we draw the line. How can we hold the belief that we can all transform and evolve, while setting boundaries that keep ourselves and our communities safe? To this day, I can't collaborate or maintain friendships with former InterVarsity staff who stayed silent, watching the organization dispose of myself and my queer students and colleagues. Even as many of them have since evolved and become LGBTQ+-affirming, it's triggering to see them on my social media feeds. While building coalitions across differences are politically essential in many contexts, we must still discern and draw boundaries to keep ourselves sane and our communities protected. How to do so from a place of connection and wisdom, rather than fear and isolation, continues to challenge me.

Kalaya'an Mendoza, director of mutual protection at Nonviolent Peaceforce, shared with me about his time supporting Indigenous leaders at Standing Rock, who held stringent expectations and standards about collaboration. The water protectors encouraged outsiders to join their movement, but were transparent about social protocols created to protect the collective, putting the onus and agency on individuals to abide by the agreed-upon standards if they wanted to support the #NoDAPL movement. These protocols included asking visitors to seriously consider their motivations for going to Standing Rock, decorum while visiting, and continuing their solidarity and learning after their visit. They cautioned visitors from coming as voyeurs, instead expecting them to contribute to the growth and safety of the community and consider how their presence, as non-Native colonial settlers, impacted the existing indigenous land, culture, and community at Standing Rock. These protocols emphasize our interconnected realities, where our presence and actions affect one another. It is up to each individual to comply with these protocols if they want to join the collective. Nobody, including and especially outsiders, can act as isolated individuals. We are all part of larger communities, histories, and legacies, which must be responsibly and carefully stewarded.

The care that Standing Rock water protectors required of outsiders shows us how the collective is always the priority, and boundaries must be honored to protect the safety of our communities and sustainability of our movements. In fact, it is these boundaries that help us hold one another accountable and protect the flourishing of the whole. Relatedly, in her distinction between activism and organizing, Mariame Kaba argues that we must organize in ways that center accountability and care for the larger collective. Kaba defines activists as individuals who are personally moved by and act on particular issues. On the other hand, organizers "can't exist solo. Because who the hell are you organizing? . . . If you're organizing, other people are counting on you, but, more importantly, your actions are accountable to someone else . . ." In *We Do This 'Til We Free Us: Abolitionist Organizing and Transformative Justice*, Kaba cautions against the individualism that can occur when activists aren't accountable to anybody, in contrast to organizing in a community context where individuals can be called out/in and held accountable by others. What each of us does as an individual matters to the whole. While InterVarsity's theological policy rollout severed the collective, accountability in community organizing is about protecting the collective.

In adrienne maree brown's *We Will Not Cancel Us*, disposability politics is tied to the destructive power of punitive justice, whereby "a wide variety of harm doing gets collapsed into one label of bad, disposable person/organization and receives one punishment: a call out, often for some form of instant cancelation." brown explains that the instant judgment and punishment unleashed in cancel culture are punitive practices of power over others. Often, our approaches to difference and conflict get reduced to these carceral logics. Out of fear, we try to "clarify an enemy, a someone outside of ourselves to blame, who is guilty, who is the origin of harm," and we banish them from the community, as if we are not also capable of that harm. Disposability, distinct from accountability, often becomes the thing we are simultaneously combating, internalizing, and practicing.

It wasn't until I moved to Texas when I more seriously confronted my own disposability politics. When I first relocated, it was easy to critique, often from the safe distance of my screen, the political strategies and messages I didn't agree with. On the one-year anniversary of the Atlanta spa mass shooting, several local Asian American organizations and politicians organized a vigil to honor and remember the victims. I volunteered to do a reading at the vigil, not knowing the politics of the other speakers and organizers of the event. To my surprise, the event showcased mostly male speakers, one of them leading us to "applaud the police officers who keep us safe" from anti-Asian hate. Another speaker proclaimed how we as

Asian Americans deserve safety because "we've proven we're model Americans." I cringed and found their messages not only unproductive but assimilationist and violent. I read my piece, left early, and, as I do, took to Twitter. In voicing my tension about the event, I made a desperate cry for help looking for Houston-based Asian American abolitionists who were as disturbed by the event as I was.

Shortly after the tweet, I got connected with Steven Wu, an abolitionist organizer with Woori Juntos, working to ensure language access to Asian and immigrant communities in Texas. Wu introduced me to a community of leftist Asian Americans in Houston, perturbed by Texas politics and actively organizing among the complicated, increasingly fascist political landscape. The group met, read books together, and started building relationships with each other. Our group of forty-six (and growing) has become a space to organize political education reading groups, share resources and mutual aid requests, attend protests together, support one another's work, and coordinate responses to local and state policies.

As somebody new to Texas politics, I find myself looking to this group and other organizers to teach me how to survive, strategize, and build community in a state that often feels dystopian in its racist, anti-immigrant, antiabortion, anti-CRT, anti-queer and -trans political backdrop. In the group, we come from different backgrounds, ages, and expertise, and yet all are working to build a leftist political home in their respective contexts. In a state that weaponizes and manufactures hysteria around platforms like "defund the police" and "critical race theory," I've seen members of this group strategize carefully to

mobilize their communities, especially intergenerational immigrant communities, without diluting their politics.

Through this group, I was recommended by Wu to apply
to the city of Houston's first Asian American Pacific Islander
Advisory Board to advise the city's mayor on issues that concern
the AAPI Houston community, including data disaggregation,
language access, anti-Asian hate, and civic engagement, among
other issues. In an information meeting about the advisory
board, I recognized the facilitator as one of the speakers from
the Atlanta vigil. The mayor's office wanted to create an advisory
board that was bipartisan, including representation of AAPI
Republicans and business leaders. During my interview, I was
told that I would "have the opportunity through the advisory
board to work with government institutions like the Houston
Police Department." I rolled my eyes over the phone. I have no
desire to work with cops, and am rarely, if ever, in conversation
with AAPI Republicans and business leaders.

I previously would have never considered moving forward
with this process after learning the advisory board would work
with law enforcement. And yet, I remembered I applied for
this position to try to ensure representation of abolitionist
voices on the board, which undoubtedly would require collaboration across political differences *and* unwavering commitment to a leftist vision for Houston. Since relocating to
Texas, I've witnessed Ethnic Studies organizers strategically
collaborate with constituents who do not always have the same
politics. Even when I disagree with certain partnerships, or
worry that Ethnic Studies might get diluted by these collab-
orations to be more palatable, I respect local organizers and

their chosen strategies. I am not the one working overtime to mobilize AAPI youth and families to get Ethnic Studies in our classrooms; they are. I trust and look to local organizers as my teachers, as I learn to let go, little by little, of my own ideological purity and arrogance.

As Grace Lee Boggs noted, dramatic and systemic change begins with critical connections, not necessarily critical mass. Sometimes, this connection means working through our differences. In *The Next American Revolution: Sustainable Activism for the Twenty-First Century*, Boggs wrote, "Struggle doesn't always have to be confrontational but can take the form of reaching out to find common ground with the many 'others' in our society who are also seeking ways out from alienation, isolation, privatization, and dehumanization by corporate globalization." Community and connection are worth struggling for, "because community is the most important thing that has been destroyed by the dominant culture" that prioritizes bureaucratic, patriarchal, and economic domination. This concept and practice of community is what rehumanizes me, reconnects me to the larger collective, and gives me hope after being disposed of by InterVarsity. This vision of community is what I fight for and invite others into.

Disposability politics facilitates transactional solidarity, which Desis Rising Up and Moving describes as "You show up for us and we'll show up for you."[1] Kaba, however, writes about bringing others into the fold of our communities and movements sustainably: "I believe we need more people all the time in all of our work, in all of our movements, in all of our struggles. The question is how do we get folks to struggle alongside us and with us. . . . What are points of entry for people, so that they can find a way to lend what they know how to do, their talent, their ideas to whatever it is that we're doing, while also learning the process?" Rather than reducing solidarity to extractive, transferable exchanges, our collective survival depends on creating on-ramps for more of us to get politicized and involved in building a better world together. While disposability politics have "traumatized and socialized us away from interdependence," transformative relationships and invitations described by Kaba generate hospitality, evolution, and growth in our movements. This does not mean watering down our politics. It means taking unwavering stances on issues that matter to the survival of our communities, while creating irresistible[2] onramps for more to lend their strengths, resources, and passions to our movements.

Texas, where it often feels like ground zero for critical battles over our rights, has taught me that the more extreme the political context, the more we truly need each other. I can't always afford to dispose of people and opportunities I disagree with. Instead of writing one another off so easily, as I once did out of my own fear and pain, Boggs, Kaba, and brown challenge us to become responsible for one another and accountable to our movements by engaging generatively through conflict and difference, beyond disposability. As we continue to witness state violence, repression, and the limitations of our institutions, we must learn to critically connect across differences and organize community infrastructure (that doesn't rely on the state) to bring in and protect one another.

•••

CULTIVATING INTENTIONAL COMMUNITY WITH EACH OTHER
and actively contributing to a collective that holds us accountable helps us "not only imagine new worlds, but also imagine ourselves differently." For this reason, Boggs often wrote
about the centrality of spirituality in social movements. For
Boggs, spirituality was a practice of compassion toward ourselves and others. Because we are often entangled in the very
logics and systems we are organizing to change, spirituality is
an outlet that facilitates transformation of the self. Similarly,
Kaba writes, "White supremacy, misogyny, ableism, classism,
homophobia, and transphobia exist everywhere. We have all
so thoroughly internalized these logics of oppression that if
oppression were to end tomorrow, we would be likely to reproduce previous structures."[3] Spirituality helps us surrender our
egos, so that we may unlearn the logics of oppression and
awaken to the divinity within all of us, ultimately educing a
leap of faith in what it means to be human.

Leaving InterVarsity required my own leap of faith in
reimagining my role in movements differently. While my
younger self longed to stay to support my queer students and
colleagues, my queerness demanded room to breathe. My
full humanity became incompatible with evangelical spaces,
and my physical and mental health suffered as I endured
noxious, inane conversations with homophobic supervisors
and peers. It didn't matter whether individuals were ambivalent or adversarial; the structure was spiritually violent and
poisoned all of my interpersonal interactions. At the rate I
was advocating—and in doing so, putting myself in harm's

way—I was en route to disposing myself if they didn't do it for me. And yet it felt impossible to leave to preserve myself. I believed I had to personally suffer for our cause.

Tarango-Sho describes this martyrdom—the way we believe it is up to us to make things happen in social justice work—as an internalized sense of American exceptionalism in our own theologies. While this may be true in some contexts, we are rarely "the only one." There is community beyond the individual, including our ancestors and descendants. And there is a timeline for change beyond the immediate. In the midst of our struggle with InterVarsity, I organized a gathering for queer students at our Northern California conference. We went around to introduce ourselves, and almost every student shared about challenging their ministers—my coworkers—on their own campuses to confront and reconsider the forthcoming policy on sexuality. As I sat and listened to their pain, as well as their insights and strategies, I began to feel lighter. It was like they came around me and affirmed, "We got this. You can go now." I didn't need to personally take every single blow anymore because we were a community. I could leave to take care of myself, and this fight wouldn't end with me. Despite how alienated I felt in my organization, there was a community of queer students beside me and behind me, with more energy and creativity. These younger queers had it handled. I could leave and heal.

I do not know what faith looks like after InterVarsity, but spirituality has never left me. In fact, it has become inextricable to my politics and my understanding of the interconnected collective. Traditional Chinese Medicine, which I sought out to address the chronic back pain I developed in InterVarsity, has become a vehicle to reclaim my own indigenous spiritual frameworks and knowledge systems. Often, I book a session expecting to address one symptom, and my body communicates new insights to me and my acupuncturist. I once wrote on an appointment intake form, "I need help with sleeplessness and fatigue." In our session, my acupuncturist read my pulse, which indicated that my lungs were struggling. In Traditional Chinese Medicine, the lungs are connected to grief, and I had been unknowingly holding my breath all week after hearing my best friend was having suicidal thoughts. She administered healing lung points, and I spent the session breathing, moving, and working through my sorrow and fear for my friend. Through acupuncture, my body reminded me that my friend and I are interconnected, and our bodies are intertwined in relationship with each other and the broader community. Traditional Chinese Medicine, with its own intricate intelligence, heals and grounds me through connection.

Acupuncture also opens up channels for me to communicate with the divine, and my practitioner often activates points for me to receive wisdom and inspiration from ancestors to support my creative processes. Acupuncture, along with feng shui, astrology, herbalism, ancestral veneration, and other indigenous spiritual traditions and knowledge systems, have all been devalued and stigmatized by Western Christian frameworks. In *Healing Justice Lineages*, Black queer feminist Erica Woodland writes, "Many of us do not actually know the spiritual practices of our ancestors due to the legacy of colonization, genocide, and enslavement. These ancestral traditions were instrumental guides for our people to address suffering as well as to help us individually and collectively connect with Spirit, our true nature, and our destiny on Earth." In her essay "Return to Spirit: Lineage, Integrity, and Accountability," Woodland identifies Christian supremacy, colluding with White supremacy and capitalism, as consistently co-opting, commodifying, demonizing, criminalizing, and erasing our spiritual traditions.

In my own evangelical religious socialization, I learned to fear my own family's traditions. The compulsory nature of assimilation, heightened by participation in Christianity, can make it challenging to trace back our ancestral practices. Growing up, I heard Chinese American evangelicals categorize ancestor veneration as "idol worship," in the same classification as "heathenism." Thus, receiving monthly acupuncture and even creating my own ancestral altar at home have become indigenizing spiritual practices for me of remembrance, reconnecting me to my community, ancestry, and the divine.

For Asian Americans trying to leave evangelical spaces, it can feel easier to follow the road map of White ex-evangelicals or even the history of Asian American churches in the US than to reconnect with our ancestral traditions. And yet, while evangelicalism, assimilation, and imperialism have shut the door to our own practices, for many of us, we actually can re-open that door. Jeanelle Nicolas Abiola, a Filipinx faith-based organizer and pastor, shares, "It's sad to let immigration and assimilation separate us from generations of indigenous culture that have lasted and survived before us." Many of us still have access to elders, motherlands, and our own decolonial (un)learning.

Admittedly, exploring Chinese cultural practices that evangelicals have deemed illegitimate and demonic is liberatory in theory, but can feel awkward in practice. Because I grew up rejecting a lot of these traditions, it feels intimidating to return to them. And yet, through community leaders and elders teaching me, I've learned to follow my intuition and appropriate these practices in ways that feel authentic to me. Reverend Deborah Lee, an immigrant rights organizer and pastor in the Bay Area, has been practicing tai chi for decades. In a community tai chi session she facilitated, she incorporated tai chi as we took turns verbalizing prayers, manifestations, and affirmations for our communities, much like corporate prayer I experienced in church services. As we inhaled, we invited in ancestral and divine wisdom. As we exhaled, we named specific prayers and manifestations for others, from safety for migrants at the US-Mexico border to protection for abortion seekers and providers. I do not know if traditional tai chi typically involves speaking, much less corporate prayer, but the moment was revelatory for me. Her practice helped attune us to our bodies, one another, and the larger movements and communities we are part of. Cultural practices are not stagnant, but can adapt and change across generations according to what we need and have access to at any given moment. And, when pursued in community under the invitation of practitioners, elders, and spiritual guides who come from the specific spiritual and cultural traditions, these practices can feel less intimidating and more accessible.

For a time, Abiola felt like they had to choose between Christianity or their own indigenous culture, but indigenous wisdom was not completely erased when Christianity came, it was just expressed differently: "I believe that's why you see different types of Christianity and Catholicism in different countries. There are different things that resonate. For example, not everyone has a baby Jesus, but we do, and I feel like that's tied to something in us before Christianity." Part of Abiola's decolonial journey involves remembering and reconnecting with the Filipinx diaspora and homeland: "I'm only one generation removed from being birthed at home, growing my own food, Filipino being my main language. I see Asian Americans thirst for this reconnection to our cultures, but for many of us, our homeland is still there, waiting for us. *We're in diaspora, we don't have to be American.*"

Reconnecting with our ancestral homelands, indigenous wisdom, and diasporic communities are part of what Mendoza describes as cultivating hope where we are now, "in the heart of empire": "We can look to our relatives back home, as well as our ancestral technologies and gifts, to teach us how to survive and navigate fascism. Our ancestors have survived occupation, genocide, colonization. Yes, we've inherited trauma, but we've also inherited their community and joy and strategies. It's in our DNA." One of the things humans do consistently is build communities, and Mendoza explains we have historically relied on community as an antidote to violence and isolation. While we face everyday horrors and failures of the state, we also resist through everyday, loving acts of care and kinship. These dualities have always coexisted. Similarly, Kaba reflects on Sonia Sanchez, who encourages us to "call on our residual memories" and turn to our ancestors to help us navigate our present-day political struggles. Kaba writes, "[Sanchez] is speaking about the importance of spirituality, in whatever form it might manifest for you. We must hear the voices and have the dreams of those who came before us, and we must keep them with us in a very real sense. This will keep us centered."[4]

The more fascist state violence escalates, the more we must rely on spirituality to ground us in our interconnectedness. Boggs regularly opened up meetings and conversations by posing the question, "What time is it on the clock of the world?" This question implores us to consider social conditions in other parts of the world, and to see our linkages with all beings. During the US-funded genocide of Palestinians in 2023, when many of us witnessed the mass displacement, maiming, torture, rape, and murder of Palestinians by Israel (while others of us looked away), I found my need for spirituality reawakened. As an American citizen and taxpayer, I was inextricably linked to the genocide of Palestinians because I helped to fund it. In my disgust and shame, I joined the majority of the world boycotting, protesting, calling and emailing our representatives, and sharing updates on social media. And still the West supplied and supported Israel's escalating war crimes, all the while intensifying repression and police violence against those who protested the genocide domestically. Nothing I could do could absolve my inherent complicity as an American, and I felt my need for God on a guttural level.

In this time, I found God trapped and dismembered under rubble. I found God with the children shaking in shock with ashen faces stained with blood. I found God filling the mass grave with body bags upon body bags. Juxtaposed to the incomprehensible extent of death and dehumanization, I also found God among the Palestinian men who stayed behind to dig one another's kin out of the rubble. I found God among the elderly, the children, and the amputees, moving slowly with one another so nobody got left behind, despite the urgency to flee for their lives. In the face of the disposability and violence, I found God in the ways Palestinians valued and protected the preciousness of human life. And this God incarnate helped me endure, in hope and action for a liberated Palestine.

THE CONCEPT OF DISPOSABILITY POLITICS, AS CONCEPTUALized by disability justice advocates, teaches us that our different bodies and social locations determine not only our chances of survival but the worth society ascribes to us. Awaiting natural disasters, disability justice activist and author Leah Lakshmi Piepzna-Samarasinha worries that she, among sick and disabled people, "will be the ones abandoned when our cities flood." In *Care Work: Dreaming Disability Justice*, she writes, "We have been thrown away by so many people. We try not to throw each other away." Keeping each other in the fold of connection and community, then, is the panacea to the dangerous dehumanization of disposability.

When Boggs asked, "What time is it on the clock of the world?" she also emphasized, "The world is always being made and never finished." Indeed, the clock of the world is still ticking, and we are called upon to make the spiritual leap beyond the urgency, individualism, and disposability toward a more abundant and interconnected understanding of humanity. Boggs stressed the significance of community over and over again, and practiced this by creating and encouraging new forms of community-based institutions, including community gardens, coops, and community development associations, that give us ownership and help us ensure the well-being of the community and environment. Relying on each other, rather than White supremacist structures and institutions, is more and more critical as political, humanitarian, and environmental crises unfold.

"Normally it would take decades for a people to transform themselves from the hyperindividualist, hypermaterialist, damaged human beings that Americans in all walks of life are today to the loving, caring people we need in the deepening crises. But these are not normal times. If we don't speed up this transformation, the likelihood is that, armed with AK-47s, we will soon be at one another's throats," Boggs wrote. The times have never been "normal," and this moment insists we not only struggle against injustice, but create, love, and care for one another radically. In Boggs's ever-prescient words, it is time to make the philosophical and spiritual leap to become more "human" human beings. "These are the times to grow our souls."[5]

ancestor altar

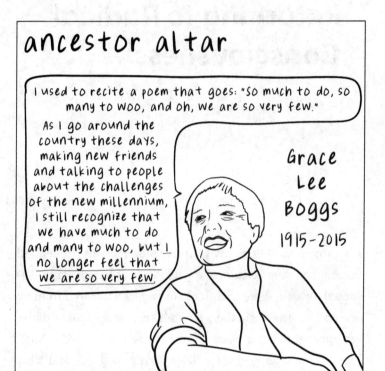

I used to recite a poem that goes: "So much to do, so many to woo, and oh, we are so very few."

As I go around the country these days, making new friends and talking to people about the challenges of the new millennium, I still recognize that we have much to do and many to woo, but I no longer feel that we are so very few.

Grace Lee Boggs

1915-2015

7

Asian Diaspora: Returning to Radical Consciousness

I became a mother as my country's government funded, endorsed, and even celebrated the genocide of Palestinians. As I rocked my own three-month-old to sleep, I witnessed from my screen Palestinian mothers snuggle their stiff, dead children, wrapped in delicate white sheets stained with blood. Much like me, they hugged their babies, sang to them, and whispered prayers in their ears, but their eyes stared blankly ahead, empty of life and pregnant with death. I awoke throughout the night to the cries of my son, which became fewer and farther in between as the months went on. "We're lucky he lets us sleep!" I texted my friends checking in on me. Seconds later, I would open social media and awaken again, in a new way, to the cries of Palestinians dying to the backdrop of bomb after bomb after bomb, striking down neighborhoods, schools, places of worship, hospitals, refugee camps, and "safe routes." As I anticipated my baby's next wake window, I witnessed Palestinian babies who would never wake again. Orange missiles momentarily lit up the smoke-filled skies as Gaza fell back under the heavy cloaks of darkness, while Israel pulled electricity and communications so they could murder without witnesses.

My first day back from maternity leave was twelve hours long. In between meetings, I ached for my baby. After nine months of carrying him around campus to classes and meetings with him in my belly, I was now back again, a new person on the same campus. I checked in with our nanny when I noticed a text from my friend that twenty-four of her family members had been murdered by Israel. They'd left their lives and ancestral home in Gaza and retreated south for safety, as they were instructed to do, when they were bombed. I considered pausing the chitchat in our graduate student offices to acknowledge what happened, but my colleagues' conversation moved too fast, and my grief-stricken mom brain lagged behind. I returned to my meetings with my research team, where we reviewed papers written by peers on religious discrimination, specifically Islamophobia and anti-Semitism. Nobody mentioned the genocide, nor the murder of Palestinian American six-year-old Wadea al-Fayoume in Plainfield, Illinois, who was stabbed twenty-six times by his landlord, nor the fatal stabbing of Detroit synagogue president Samantha Woll outside her home, all of which happened within days of our meeting. The two times I brought up Palestine, the facilitator looked at me like he would break out into hives. This first day back drained me, trying to function and produce as the cords of grief and love—heavily, forcefully—pulled me to my baby and to Gaza. I found myself again in an institution that ignored injustice, that expected us to pretend our hearts were not breaking and ethnic cleansing was not occurring before our eyes.

At this time, I also started my two-year assignment as a board member to an Asian American community organization and paid close attention to the responses of the AAPI nonprofit world. I was ignorant to assume it would be a no-brainer for organizations serving our communities to put out statements of solidarity with Palestine, at the very least. The central role of the US in the systematic displacement and extermination of Palestinians is obvious (the receipts have been there for decades), yet the issue was contentious. Those calling for a ceasefire got censored, doxxed, and harassed, a phenomenon backing many of us into fear—of losing funding, of losing supporters—rather than compelling us into moral courage and action. While a handful of Asian American organizations were vocal to support Palestinian-led efforts and issued unwavering statements of solidarity and calls to action, others remained silent. There were statements condemning Islamophobia and anti-Semitism, but statements explicitly naming genocide, settler colonialism, and decolonial solidarity were fewer and farther in between.

"I feel an unease within Asian Americanness. We don't have a common understanding of who we are, who we belong to, or who belongs to us," Jeanelle Abiola shared with me over Zoom a few months prior to the genocide. Indeed, the term "Asian American" encompasses over fifty ethnic groups speaking over one hundred languages, often privileging East Asians and erasing Southeast Asians, undocumented Asians, queer and trans Asians, among other marginalized Asian subgroups. As demonstrated by the "Asian American" label, racial identity is an ongoing—often contentious—process of boundary expansion and constriction, reactive to immigration waves, policies, social movements, and geopolitics.

The Asian American movement in the late 1960s wrestled with questions of who we are, who we belong to, and who belongs to us in the context of the antiwar movement. As the country witnessed the atrocities and bloodshed of American intervention throughout the Global South during the Cold War, anticolonial indignation became central to the formation of Asian American identity and politics. The war in Vietnam in particular was a "brutal and urgent politicization."[1] To identify as Asian American at the time was to be unapologetically critical of the US empire and to fight for liberation and self-determination in solidarity with Black, Brown, and Indigenous peoples at home and abroad.

The term "Asian American" was an active refusal of the externally imposed colonial label "Oriental." Edward Said, a Palestinian academic, political activist, and one of the founders of postcolonial studies, coined the term "Orientalism" in 1978 to explain the West's fictitious construction of Southwest Asia and North Africa as primitive, static, despotic, perpetually foreign, and objectified. These orientalist representations depended on and upheld Western colonial regimes in the region financially, culturally, and institutionally. Ideological conquest is waged alongside military conquest, where difference is regarded as a threat that must be contained or destroyed. Thus, Orientalism has racist, violent, and at times genocidal implications.

Said's theoretical framework was soon adopted by East and South Asians in the US to describe their experiences domestically and internationally as well. The Asian American movement argued that to reject the dehumanizing and infantilizing identity of "Oriental" and assert Asian American subjectivity on one's own terms also required a rejection of the US imperialist system that laid the foundation for Orientalism, anti-Asian racism, and White supremacy at home and abroad. However, as scholars like Dr. Najwa Mayer called out in the 2024 Association for Asian American Studies (AAAS) conference, many Asian American scholars and activists today benefit from Said's work without reckoning with the material conditions of colonization that foreground his scholarship.

Mobilized by revolutionary decolonial movements in the Global South, Asian Americans in the antiwar movement defined pan-Asian political identity through diasporic solidarity with the Third World majority confronting the brutalities of colonialism. The Pilipinx American Collegiate Endeavor (PACE), one of the founding groups of the Third World Liberation Front at San Francisco State University, wrote in 1968: "So we have decided to fuse ourselves with the masses of Third World people, which are the majority of the world's people, to create, through struggle, a new humanity, a new humanism, a New World Consciousness, and within that context collectively control our own destinies."[2] With Asians across the globe impacted and displaced by US imperialism, Asian American as a political identity was not a US-centric demographic category, but an internationalist political identity that facilitated pan-Asian solidarity among different Asian subgroups in the US, as well as with anticolonial movements around the world. To be Asian American was to fight for liberation and self-determination in the US and in the Global South, critiquing the violent arms of the US empire domestically as well as in Southeast Asia, Africa, and Latin America during the Cold War. Asian American political identity contributed to the evolution of a new humanity that honored and defended our interconnected, decolonial struggles.

Alex Hing, one of the founders of the Red Guards, a Bay Area Asian American revolutionary organization modeled after the Black Panthers, wrote in "The Need for a United Asian American Front" in 1970: "We are Asians, and as such, identify ourselves with the baddest motherfuckers alive. We can no longer be a witness to the daily slaughter of our people in Asia nor to the oppression of the Asians here in America and be afraid of death or prison. We must fight because that's what Asians are all about." As a rallying cry for a pan-Asian front, Hing referenced the violence Asians in their home countries and Asians in the US suffered at the hands of the US military and police. Asian American soldiers, for example, often faced racist abuse in the military during the Vietnam War, hearing profanities like "We kill people who look like you!" from military leaders. In *Asian American Histories of the United States,* historian Catherine Ceniza Choy writes, "The horror of witnessing and participating in violence against people who bore a resemblance to their own families took a psychological toll." Asian experiences domestically and internationally were connected by the violence of empire, intertwining Asian American identity to the Third World global majority.

Asian American women at the time joined feminist scholars and activists in the Global South, turning to revolutionary women in Asia as political role models and dialogue partners. Together, they cultivated Third World feminist critiques of the US empire and militarism, sexuality and reproduction, capitalism, and patriarchy. Central to this racial project was the evocation of Asian women as sexual objects, operationalized through fetishizing stereotypes and the systematic creation of red-light districts in Asian countries with US troops. Sociologist Joane Nagel coins the institutionalized practice of American GIs frequenting Asian sex workers the "military sexual complex," which has always been integral to military culture, practice, and discourse within and beyond Asia.[3] Historian Judy Tzu-Chun Wu writes, "The [US] military produced and relied on anti-Asian racial hatred toward Asians to motivate US soldiers to fight in Asia, carrying out anti-Asian racial attitudes back and forth across the Pacific."[4] Understanding how colonial violence and sexist, racial subjugation traveled and reinforced itself across the Pacific, Asian American feminists refused to separate themselves from their Asian counterparts. "Racism against them is too often racism against us," wrote Evelyn Yoshimura, a Japanese American activist.[5]

Black and Asian solidarity was also central to the anti-imperialist politics of the Asian American movement. Black and Asian American groups were both recruited and deployed by the US military-industrial complex to fight imperialist wars on the front lines. They opposed US military intervention in Vietnam and elsewhere as the number of US casualties and federal government war expenditures soared. Both groups were inspired by and in solidarity with Third World national liberation movements throughout Africa, Asia, and Latin America, which ranged from anticolonial wars for independence from European control, as in Algeria, to revolutions that fundamentally changed systems and institutions within their societies, such as in Cuba during the 1950s.[6] Historian Vijay Prashad names this "internationalist nationalism" of solidarity among those fighting against imperialism around the world, where racialized groups in the US drew upon the inspiration, theoretical frameworks, and political critiques of Third World peoples and maintained reciprocal relationships of material support with other national liberation movements.[7]

In addition to antiwar organizing, Black and Asian communities organized domestically over shared struggles. Police consistently harassed Chinatown youth, and the Black Panther Party (BPP) facilitated political education sessions with them, introducing them to the BPP ten-point program. When Chinatown youth asked to join the BPP, Bobby Seale, political activist and BPP cofounder, replied, "No, you've got to form your own group, grounded in your own struggle."[8] The distinctions between Black and Asian racialized experiences mattered, so Chinese American youth soon formed the San Francisco Red Guards in 1969, merging with I Wor Kuen of New York two years later. The group served as a radical Asian American youth organizing collective and political home that worked in solidarity with the BPP and the Puerto Rican Young Lords Party. They mobilized Asian Americans to oppose capitalism, racism, and heteropatriarchy in the US and around the world.[9]

Led by women at the center of leadership, exposing the racist imperialist nature of the US empire was central to the Red Guards' revolutionary agenda. Pam Tau Lee, one of the feminist youth organizers, wrote, "For me and so many others, 'All power to the people' also meant being internationalists." Moved by the Black Panther Party, they wrote their own twelve-point platform grounded in the Asian American experience, where international solidarity was a major tenet: "We want self-determination for all Asians. Western imperialists have been invading and colonizing countries in Asia for the past 500 years. Amerikan imperialism, concentrating in Asia, is now engaged in the most sadistic [and environmentally destructive—Agent Orange] and genocidal war of aggression the world has ever seen. We want an immediate end to Amerikan imperialism."[10]

Given such forthright calls for internationalist, interracial solidarity against imperialism, how are the ties between Asian American, antiracist, and anticolonial struggles so ambiguous today? As demonstrated throughout this book, our responses to social movements against injustice have been cacophonous. How did the questions of who we are, who we belong to, and who belongs to us shrink from a capacious solidarity that transgresses racial and international borders, to insular arguments about representation and inclusion into the imperialist state? Why, in times of crisis, do Asian American so-called leaders urge us to prove our Americanness, when the moment demands us to indict America and refuse its violent agenda altogether?

Native Hawai'ian scholars Stephanie Nohelani Teves and Maile Arvin explain that the White supremacist structure in the US rewards Asian Americans for "civic participation and cultural assimilation" into its institutions, "while ignoring the genocide and slavery upon which their aspirations for inclusion depend."[11] As Native Hawai'ian educator and activist Haunani-Kay Trask pointed out, the political agenda for Asian

Americans has generally meant "a bigger piece of the American pie," but "cooked from a recipe of [Native] displacement and dispossession."[12] Asian Americans are racialized and assimilated in ways that reward proximity to Whiteness and erase Indigenous claims, which are critical to the US settler colonial project.[13]

Because of fundamental ideological differences, political coalitions between Asian Americans and Pacific Islanders are difficult to form and maintain, and there have been tensions as the groups are often amalgamated together in the broad NHAAPI (Native Hawai'ian Asian American Pacific Islander) category. Pacific Islander struggles for sovereignty, as well as Women of Color feminisms, frame "the state as a site of violence, not resolution."[14] This is often at odds with Asian American liberal politics that understand the state as a site for greater recognition and inclusion. While many Asian Americans work to gain seats in the US system and make it work for us, Indigenous struggles for sovereignty and decolonization are struggles to survive colonial domination and genocide under that same US system. Asian American liberal politics of inclusion into the US may not only conflict with the radical politics of liberation and decolonization but depend on violent settler colonial logics. The irony is that many of us are here *because* of American imperialism and interventions in our home countries, via forced or voluntary migration. Thus, Asian American solidarity with decolonial movements, from Hawai'i to Palestine, necessitates a reckoning with our own—often painful and contradictory—relationships to the US empire, and our own status as settlers on and benefactors of stolen Indigenous land.

I'm often ambivalent about the terms "Asian American" and "AAPI," as many are. Some are eager to use it as a tool to advocate for more representation in mainstream institutions, like politics, business, and Hollywood. Others reject it and find it irrelevant, arguing that it flattens specificities and holds little meaning compared to their ethnic identities. Still, some utilize the term to honor legacies of the Asian American movement and to galvanize their communities around interracial, anti-imperialist, anticapitalist coalitions. In his talk "On the Death of Asian Americans," novelist and professor Viet Thanh Nguyen keenly notes, "The incoherence of Asian America lies in the gap between the acceptable politics of inclusion and limited solidarity and the potentially more radical politics of expansive solidarity." Indeed, this gap reflects the "instability at the heart of Asian Americanness," as identified by journalist Jeff Chang in *We Gon' Be Alright: Notes on Race and Resegregation*. The term "Asian American" is contentious and no longer synonymous with radical politics as it once was. In fact, writer Jay Caspian Kang even reduces the elicitation of 1960s Asian American radical politics to an act of nostalgia. In the ongoing, unsettled creation and re-creation of Asian American identity, I return to Abiola's questions: *Who are we? Who do we belong to? Who belongs to us?*

MY CHILD'S CHINESE NAME, 家衍 GA-YIN, WAS GIVEN TO HIM BY my mother. Just as I was named by my grandmother, I wanted my son to be named by his. 家衍 "Ga-Yin" holds a double meaning: "to take an expansive view of family," and "to embody an indomitable spirit." My mother gave him this Chinese name without knowing that we had also given him the Filipino name Kapwa, the indigenous Tagalog word for "people of shared identity and belonging," or "my other me." We chose Kapwa because it reflects our deepest longing not only for our child but for humanity. "Kapwa" embodies our interconnections and our prayer to live into our true belonging to each other, where your pain is my pain, your liberation is my liberation, and you are my other me. Unintentionally, 家荷 Ga-Yin Kapwa's names complement each other.

I experienced kapwa firsthand through the care I received from my mother during my postpartum period. I had an unexpectedly traumatic birth. Intervention after intervention, followed by complication after complication, I hallucinated and disassociated for the first day of my baby's life. I lost so much blood and felt so violated by medical professionals during labor and delivery that my brain went into survival mode. I spoke nonsensically as a means of self-preservation. When doctors and nurses asked me if I knew where I was, I told them I was in Taiwan. Unconsciously, I threw chaos at them to shield myself and my family from more of their aggression. I refused to let them access any more of us, and my own consciousness became my weapon. They thought I had gone insane and ordered an emergency psychiatry consultation.

When my parents arrived two days later, I slowly started returning back to myself. In the midst of claustrophobic tubes, needles, blood transfusions, and CT scans, seeing my parents was my first time I exhaled during the whole ordeal. It took months before I fully landed back into myself and regained a sense of safety. There were days I thought I would never get better. I couldn't walk, I couldn't wipe my own ass, I couldn't nurse, I couldn't even hold or feed my child. They had taken too much from me. For the following thirty tender yet tumultuous days of early motherhood, my mother lived with us as I healed emotionally and physically. She cooked for me around the clock. I had to take medicine every six hours, but it couldn't be on an empty stomach, so she made me ground pork congee at one in the morning. She washed my baby's bottles until her back hurt from standing for so long. She grocery shopped, did the laundry, yelled at me for not wearing socks, and took care of our dogs even though she hates pets. I was agonized over receiving this much help, to which she replied, "I wish you loved yourself more."

Parental love is some of the wildest, most connective love. She flew home after the month of taking care of me and my family and ended up in the emergency room once she returned due to an allergic reaction. She broke out into hives that plagued her for weeks; the cause is unknown to this day. I wondered if her body paid the price from the stress of caretaking around the clock and worrying about my postpartum complications. My pain was her pain. Her body communicated a solidarity that transcended words. We remain interconnected.

Who are we? Who do we belong to? Who belongs to us? On my first day back on campus, my body was in the sociology building, but my heart longed for my baby and ached for my friend's family in Gaza. They remain my other me. Where Orientalism, imperialism, and racial categories separate us, kapwa, 家荷 Ga-Yin, and parental love brought me into a new consciousness about the collective. Kapwa implies we belong not to America, but to each other, in the diaspora and with other diasporic peoples. 家荷 Ga-Yin calls me to an expansive view of family beyond bloodlines and borders, and to stand in solidarity with an indomitable spirit. In this particular historical moment of social movements and revolutions, I offer my son's namesake as our guide to iterating the Asian American label. I propose Asian Diaspora, grounded in kapwa and 家荷 Ga-Yin, as the next political identity to meet the demands and possibilities of this generation, bringing us together into diasporic, antiracist, anti-imperialist collective love that refuses to abet the American empire.

Diaspora extends to a range of cultural and geographical contexts, but one core characteristic of diaspora is the experience of not being fully accepted by your host land. Generally, diaspora refers to the migration of formerly colonized peoples to the West, at times accompanied by the weakening of the nation-state and the displacement of people because of imperialist intervention and transnational flows of capital and labor. However, diaspora may also be appropriated by groups who do not experience forced dispersion, don't share the longing to return to homeland, and may shuttle between homeland and host land in a continuous fashion. Thus, the diaspora includes the immigrant, the expatriate, the refugee, the migrant worker, the exiled, and ethnic and racial communities who experience exclusion from the West.

Kwok Pui-lan writes in *Postcolonial Imagination and Feminist Theory* that diaspora is an increasingly global and common phenomenon "because of cultural and economic regrouping after decolonization, forced or voluntary migration, and transnational linkages in an age of global capitalism, communications, and transport." The Asian Diaspora is a fluid site that challenges the construction of the US as the center. With flows of capital, culture, and communication between Asian immigrants, their homelands, and Asian diasporic peoples, the Asian Diaspora is constantly reconfiguring home and transgressing borders. As demonstrated by the ethnoburb and its supportive transnational networks, assimilation and allegiance to Whiteness are not the final destination. Instead, diaspora asserts multiple loyalties and identities, as well as various definitions and experiences of home, borders, and displacement. Asian diasporic consciousness is simultaneously "here" and "there," renegotiating, shifting, changing contexts, and expanding.[15]

Multiply-centered diasporic communities with expansive definitions of home learn from each other to forge new political identities and coalitions.[16] Much like the Third World solidarity of the late 1960s, those in the diaspora find commonality as outsiders to the American empire. Pui-lan writes, "A diasporic consciousness finds similarities and differences in both familiar territories and unexpected corners; one catches glimpses of oneself in a fleeting moment or in a fragment in someone else's story." In other words, we find ourselves in each other. This is what racially placeless Asians in the US have always done: find pieces of ourselves in the histories, cultures, stories, and art of other racialized and diasporic communities, from hip-hop to Chicano literature, because the language of the oppressed gives us categories to locate our own racialized experiences.

Similarly, Edward Said, reflecting on Italian Marxist Antonio Gramsci's *The Prison Notebooks*, insisted that we understand our histories in relation to one another's histories, in order "to become someone else, to transform [ourselves] from a unitary identity to an identity that includes the other without suppressing difference."[17] Asian diasporic political imagination recognizes ourselves in the other, a process necessary "to face new circumstances and to reinvent the identity of the people."[18] We understand ourselves in relation to each other, and we work to understand others as we'd understand ourselves. "You are my other me" midwives our individual and collective evolution.

ASIAN DIASPORA AS A POLITICAL IDENTITY ALSO COMPLICATES the framing of the US as a "nation of immigrants" and of Asian American history as a series of battles of exclusion from and inclusion into the US. Alternatively, Asian Diaspora proposes a critical examination of our relationship to empire. Rather than Asian Americans immigrating for opportunities and fighting for inclusion as the master narrative claims, historian Moon-Ho Jung argues in *Menace to Empire: Anticolonial Solidarities and the Transpacific Origins of the US Security State* that the expansion of and revolutionary resistance against the US empire conditions the experiences, migration patterns, and racialization of Asian Americans. Communities in and from Asia have historically articulated and organized revolutionary politics against the US empire. Their anti-imperialist politics threatened the US security state, serving as impetus for the US to racialize Asians as seditious threats, giving rise to immigration policies and racial categories that bolstered American imperialism. Thus, Asian American racialization is entangled in the US history of colonial conquest, White supremacy, and anticolonial struggle, particularly among the Asian Diaspora. Yellow peril and the Red Scare, for example, worked to racialize Asians as monstrous threats and, more importantly, to protect the US empire. Like Indigenous and Black subjects of the US empire, anticolonial revolutionaries in and from Asia were racialized biologically and culturally as subhuman and dangerous to justify imperial violence against them.

Exclusionary immigration policies and the racialization of Asian Americans, then, have always operated as the tools of US geopolitics and empire, as evidenced by the US's reaction to South Asian revolutionary organizing in the early 1900s. Beginning in 1913, anticolonial Bengali activists created the Ghadar ("revolt" in Urdu) newspaper and party through chapters in major universities in the West. They rallied the South Asian community, from students to agricultural and lumber mill workers, to explicitly advocate for revolution in India, by violent means if necessary. They believed in "uplifting our country from colonialism to uplift ourselves in North America." Ghadar party organizers garnered support from South Asian farmers, laborers, and elites in the diaspora. The US became the main site for organizing and promoting Indian nationalism in North America, but South Asian diasporic revolutionaries organized around the world, from Punjab to the Philippines, Hong Kong, and the San Francisco Bay Area.[19]

Ghadar Party activists who confronted the colonial state bore the brunt of US state surveillance and repression, and their anti-imperialist politics instigated South Asian exclusion in US immigration policy. Allied with the British, the US expanded state authority to monitor, exclude, and deport South Asian anticolonial activists as anarchists. South Asians became racialized as "seditious threats" to national security before and during World War I, and the US, Canada, and British governments worked together to criminalize Ghadar Party leaders. As the US closely surveilled the Ghadar Party, it became wedded to the British empire in a wider project to secure imperial borders and racial hierarchies by silencing anticolonial critiques and criminalizing anticolonial activities.[20]

Conjoining US laws on sedition and immigration with racial formation, the US turned to Orientalist racial caricatures of religious tradition, sexual deviance, and revolutionary anarchism to categorize anticolonial South Asians as unassimilable dangers to the US. San Francisco newspapers wrote, "South Asians were the most undesirable immigrants, because they were dangerous revolutionaries pledged to overthrow British domination." The US restricted South Asians from entering its borders, and from 1911 to 1915, 55 percent of all South Asian immigrants were denied (compared to 9 percent of Chinese applicants during the same years). While the British and the US formed an international alliance to defend "democracy," their treatment and racialization of anticolonial South Asians exposed that democracy was actually about securing the world order of White supremacy and the Western empire.

Asian Diaspora beckons us to carefully consider the US as a historical and ongoing empire—fueled and justified by White supremacy and the subjugation of Black and Indigenous peoples—in the racialization of our communities. Thus, the framing of the US as a nation of "immigrants" is not only incomplete but facilitates historical amnesia about our revolutionary anticolonial predecessors and encourages assimilation into US citizenry. White-washing history to construct the US as a "multicultural" nation of immigrants erases imperialism, chattel slavery, and White supremacy that made this nation possible.[21] In reality, the US state, as well as its racial categories, emerged with colonizing and racializing discourse to secure and expand empire. Through this critique of empire, we understand Asian Diaspora, and race, more broadly, not simply as a domestic matter of national exclusion or inclusion but one that emerges from the colonial origins of the US with ongoing global implications.

Because Asian Diaspora insists on anticolonial critique, the term as a political identity and organizing tool serves as a grounding principle for diasporic, decolonial solidarity against Western imperialism. By renewing our connections to our historical anticolonial rage and internationalist solidarity, Asian Diaspora reminds us that our experiences of race in the US are defined by both colonial agendas *and* anti-imperial resistance. Subsequently, we strengthen our connections to other diasporic communities on the outside of empire—including Pacific Islander and Indigenous communities—at the forefronts of resistance and struggle against imperialism and fascism. Following our revolutionary ancestors, we broaden and deepen our sense of self and solidarity across borders.

Second-generation Filipino American rapper and community worker Tim Ignacio packed up his life in the Bay Area at twenty-four years old to relocate to his ancestral homeland of the Philippines as an expression of Asian diasporic internationalist solidarity. Given the vast number of diasporic Filipinos, including his mother and lola, who were OFWs (overseas foreign workers) forced to leave the Philippines and work abroad because of imperialism, displacement, and imposed scarcity in their homeland, Ignacio understands his decision to relocate back to the Philippines as an act of decolonization and unassimilability: "So many went through so much pain to leave, so there is decolonizing work happening in the Filipino American who is able and chooses to return."

After visiting the Philippines on a solidarity trip in college and witnessing the inequalities in his homeland as legacies of Western imperialism, Ignacio questioned, "What is the right response to this injustice and to my mother's sacrifices? Is the only response just to keep climbing higher? Get even closer to Whiteness?" Witnessing the disparities between his comfortable life in the US and the street youth in Manila compelled him to identify with Filipinos in the homeland and diaspora, rather than with Americanness, "in a way that wasn't just about assimilation." Ignacio's sense of self expanded to include his kapwa in the Philippines, and spurred him to relocate indefinitely to live, work, and serve youth in urban slum communities in Metro Manila. Identifying as a balikbayan ("to return to our land"), Ignacio sees his relocation as an unassimilable iteration of Filipino diasporic identity and rejection of the so-called American Dream.

As a balikbayan, Ignacio has the opportunity to reunite with different generations of his family, meeting family members and connecting with the land through a new lens. While the US homogenizes Asians and Filipinos, his time in the Philippines helps him see and appreciate the linguistic, ethnic, and regional diversity in the country. Relearning Tagalog, he hears the distinct accents of Quezon Province, where his family is from, and questions, "How can we identify more specifically with where we're from?" In the heterogeneity among Filipinos, Ignacio says there is always a uniting tie to the land.

"Bayan" in "balikbayan" translates to "homeland," also found in "kababayan" (someone of the same land). Even in their distinctions, Ignacio as a balikbayan is connected to his kababayan because of their historical, embodied, and unbreakable ties to the land. Their differences (and Ignacio's privileges) become more apparent as he spends more time in the Philippines, yet they remain people of shared identity and land.

The late Amado Khaya Canham Rodriguez, motivated by a similar commitment to solidarity across borders, relocated from the US to the Philippines to learn, live, and advocate with the farmers and Mangyan Indigenous communities in Mindoro island. Initially a local activist in Oakland organizing against gentrification and in solidarity with the Movement for Black Lives, he became active partnering with the Filipino people in their fight for democracy in the Philippines. His activism led him back to his ancestral homeland until his untimely death on August 4, 2020, in Mindoro, Philippines. Canham Rodriguez died doing the work of building homes for the poorest of the poor in the Philippines. Contrary to what we perceive as the immigrant's American Dream, Canham Rodriguez chose the act of going back to his ancestral homeland as an expression of solidarity and love for his people, unbound by borders. In the process, he died of septic shock, likely due to food poisoning and possibly worsened by COVID-19.[22]

In his obituary, his mother, Dr. Robyn Rodriguez, wrote, "[Amado] would have said that if he died from food poisoning it is because the Filipino people—especially the Indigenous—despite being inheritors of incredibly fertile, life-giving land, live under conditions such that local landowners and foreign companies own that land. And because they do not own land, most people can barely produce enough food to eat. Amado would have said that if his death was compounded by COVID-19, it is because the Philippines—and even the United States, the country of his birth—has a health system that put profits over people."[23] In his legacy, Amado models anti-imperialist solidarity as the deepest form of diasporic love and kapwa.

Asian diasporic political identity rejects Americanness and honorary Whiteness as aspirations, and instead centers our anticolonial rage and diasporic ties to one another. At a time when the term "Asian American" is flattening, unstable, and reduced to the politics of representation and inclusion into empire, Asian Diaspora takes up the task of asserting our subjectivity to induce internationalist solidarity with anyone and everyone fighting the US empire, including decolonial movements from Palestine, Puerto Rico, the Philippines, and Hawai'i. We expand the boundaries of who belongs to us, as well as our political horizons. As part of the Asian Diaspora, we may be tempted to "enter into a settler colonial system that begs us to behave and obey like good Americans, to uphold that system rooted in genocide, slavery, patriarchy, and capitalism."[24] But as we name ourselves coconspirators against the US empire, we awaken possibilities for diasporic love, coalitions, and futures.

TO MY CHILD, BORN DURING REVOLUTION. MAY YOU AND YOUR peers know yourselves in relation to each other, becoming kapwa and practicing 家荇 Ga-Yin against empire together. Generation after generation, our call remains the same: to refuse violence and separation, to choose to belong to one another, and to evolve into more "human" human beings, as our ancestor Grace Lee Boggs prophesied.

Your auntie Jill Kunishima is a descendant of a No-No Boy. Her grandfather was apprehended by the FBI during World War II because of his Japanese ancestry, and subsequently separated from his family and placed in an incarceration camp. When given the questionnaire to prove his allegiance to the US, he became one of the twelve thousand Japanese Americans who answered "no." He refused to fight for the genocidal, warmongering country that stripped away his community's civil rights. Today, Auntie Jill's grandfather shapes her steadfast commitment to speak out against injustice. "And when I do," she says, "I always think of my grandfather, who just said 'no.'"

When the violence is too heavy for your tender heart, when the system feels too broken to comprehend, this is where you start. You say "no" to the contradictions of this country, and your refusal becomes a "yes," an opening, and the beginning of a life of decolonial solidarity and revolutionary love that will heal you from your heartache. You do not need to do more than this. And when you feel lost, return to the stories of our ethnoburb, your tito Tim and tito Amado, the San Francisco State student activists, the No-No uncles, the Palestinian mothers, the Ghadar Party revolutionaries, your great-great-grandfather, and of course my popo, our unassimilable North Star, to guide you.

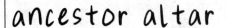

ancestor altar

The United States of America is the most powerful imperialist country in the world ... They control the United Nations. They control the Pacific Ocean—all these nuclear submarines circulating throughout the Pacific. The United States of America is a death country. It gives death to Native people. And the only way to fight the United States of America is to be political.

We are not American.

Haunani-Kay
Trask
1949–2021

Acknowledgments

Thank you, Jenny Xu, for seeing potential in me as an author before this book was even an idea. Thank you for pushing me toward clarity and confidence through my many drafts. Thank you, Tanya McKinnon, for seeing the charm of Popo's story and the vision of *Unassimilable*. Thank you for encouraging me not only to write but also to draw. Thank you, Adenike Olanrewaju, for taking on this project with enthusiasm and cheering me on to the finish line. Thank you to all three of you for your support, expertise, and most of all, warmth and hospitality in an industry that was never made for us.

Thank you to the comrades who contributed their time interviewing with me for this book: Yu Shuan Tarango-Sho, Jeanelle Abiola, Kalaya'an Mendoza, Tim Ignacio, Jill Kunishima, Erna Kim-Hackett, Liz Lin, Nate Lee, and Justin Tse. I am immensely grateful for your wisdom, your hope, your big-heartedness, your persistence, and most of all, your friendship. It was my joy to hear and receive your freedom dreams. My analysis is sharper and my heart is softer because of you all.

Thank you to my first readers and conversation partners:

Denia Perez, Angie Hong, Alicia Crosby, and AnaYelsi Velasco Sanchez. Denia, it is only fitting as my sister wife that you were the first person with whom I shared the idea of *Unassimilable*. I love how we have grown in alignment, even across distance. Angie, Alicia, and AnaYelsi, our writing group watered and nurtured *Unassimilable* when it was just a seed. I will always root for us.

Thank you to the scholar activists who empower me to pursue academia on my own terms: Drs. Russell Jeung, PEP directors (manang Arlene Daus-Magbual, manong Rod Daus-Magbual, and ate Allyson Tintiangco-Cubales), Oiyan Poon, and Anthony Ocampo. Thank you, Dr. Elaine Ecklund, for your abounding encouragement as I unconventionally wrote a book and had a baby as your advisee. Thank you Drs. Michelle Lee and christina ong, my pandemic cohort, RADAAR, and PEP. To all of you: Academia has not been the easiest time for me, but it would have been impossible without you. Thank you for making this time sweeter and lighter.

Thank you to my writer friends who demystified the writing and publishing process for me: Cinelle Barnes, Michelle Kim, and Jenny Wang. Thank you to the activists who shaped my thinking and being as I wrote: Asian Texans for Justice, Steven Wu, Makaiwa Tong, and Reverend Deborah Lee.

And to save the best for last, thank you to my family:

Thank you, Mommy and Daddy, for giving me everything. Whatever I accomplish is because of you.

Thank you, Jeff, for believing in me before I believed in myself. You are my greatest collaborator and co-conspirator, across every lifetime and every dimension. You are the dreamer and I am the manifester. We realize the impossible, together.

Thank you, Hari Kapwa, for bringing so much delight and laughter into our lives. It is my life's honor to bear witness to your becoming. I love you and will always be proud of you.

Thank you, Toro and Uni, for being my writing buddies. You kept me on schedule and offered ruthless critiques. Your comments nearly broke me, but ultimately made me better.

Thank you, Jessica, for being you. You're my chosen family so no way you're getting left out of this.

Thank you to my in-laws and our village: Lola, Lolo, and all the titas and titos who watch Hari so I have the space to do the labor of mother-scholarship.

And lastly, thank you to the divine guidance, blessing, and protection of my beloveds who became ancestors during the writing of this book: Popo, Yeye, and Babac. You are the original unassimilables. Your legacies live on.

Notes

Introduction

1. Chang, Iris. *The Chinese in America: A Narrative History.* Penguin, 2004.

2. Yang, Andrew. "Coronavirus Discrimination." *The Washington Post*, April 1, 2020, https://www.washingtonpost.com/opinions /2020/04/01/andrew-yang-coronavirus-discrimination/.

3. "Anti-Asian Hate Crime Reported to Police in America's Largest Cities: 2020." Center for the Study of Hate and Extremism, March 2020, https://www.csusb.edu/sites/default/files/FACT%20SHEET -%20Anti-Asian%20Hate%202020%203.2.21.pdf.

4. Saw, Anne, Aggie J. Yellow Horse, Russell Jeung. "Stop AAPI Hate Mental Health Report." *Stop AAPI Hate*, May 27, 2021, https:// stopaapihate.org/wp-content/uploads/2021/05/Stop-AAPI-Hate -Mental-Health-Report-210527.pdf.

5. Ibid.

6. Tachiyama, Gary, and Roland Kotani. "No-No Boys: Old and New." *The Hawaii Herald*, July 3, 1981, 1.

1 | The Ethnoburb

1. Zhou, Min. *Contemporary Chinese America: Immigration, Ethnicity, and Community Transformation.* Temple University Press, 2009: 82.

2. Lin, Mingang, and Min Zhou. "Community Transformation and the Formation of Ethnic Capital: Immigrant Chinese Communities in the United States." *Journal of Chinese Overseas* 1, no. 2 (2005): 260–84.

3. Cheng, Wendy. "The Changs Next Door to the Diazes: Suburban Racial Formation in Los Angeles's San Gabriel Valley." *Journal of Urban History* 39, no. 1 (2013): 15–35.

4. Lee, Erika. *The Making of Asian America: A History.* Simon and Schuster, 2015: 286.

5. Ibid, 290.

6. Li, Wei. "Building Ethnoburbia: The Emergence and Manifestation of the Chinese Ethnoburb in Los Angeles' San Gabriel Valley." *Journal of Asian American Studies* 2, no. 1 (1999): 1–28.

7. Cheng, Wendy. "The Changs Next Door to the Diazes: Suburban Racial Formation in Los Angeles's San Gabriel Valley." *Journal of Urban History* 39, no. 1 (2013): 15–35.

8. Zhou, Min, and Jennifer Lee. "Becoming Ethnic or Becoming American?: Reflecting on the Divergent Pathways to Social Mobility and Assimilation among the New Second Generation." *Du Bois Review: Social Science Research on Race* 4, no. 1 (2007): 189–205.

9. Horton, John. *The Politics of Diversity in Monterey Park, California.* University of Chicago Press, 1992.

10. Li, Wei. *Ethnoburb: The New Ethnic Community in Urban America.* University of Hawaii Press, 2008.

11. Zarsadiaz, James. *Resisting Change in Suburbia: Asian Immigrants and Frontier Nostalgia in LA.* Vol. 67. University of California Press, 2022.

12. Zhou, Min, Yen-Fen Tseng, and Rebecca Y. Kim. "Rethinking Residential Assimilation: The Case of a Chinese Ethnoburb in the San Gabriel Valley, California." *Amerasia Journal* 34, no. 3 (2008): 55–83.

13. Arax, Mark. "Monterey Park Asians Threaten Boycott of School." *Los Angeles Times*, November 14, 1985, https://www.latimes.com/archives/la-xpm-1985-11-14-ga-2678-story.html.

14. Horton, John. *The Politics of Diversity in Monterey Park, California.* University of Chicago Press, 1992.

2 | PWI-WAA (Predominantly White Institutions with "A Lot" of Asians)

1. Wu, Ellen. "Asian Americans Helped Build Affirmative Action. What Happened?" *Slate* (2022).

2. Lee, Sharon S. "The De-minoritization of Asian Americans: A Historical Examination of the Representations of Asian Americans in Affirmative Action Admissions Policies at the University of California." *Asian Am. LJ* 15 (2008): 129.

3. Lipsitz, George. *How Racism Takes Place.* Temple University Press, 2011.

4. Escueta, Eugenia, and Eileen O'Brien. "Asian Americans in Higher Education: Trends and Issues." *Research Briefs* 2.4 (1991): n4.

5. "Affirmative Action: History and Rationale." *The White House Archives.* Accessed April 30, 2024, https://clintonwhitehouse3 .archives.gov/WH/EOP/OP/html/aa/aao2.html.

6. Scherini, Rose, and Gregg Thomson. "Berkeley Students from 1964 to 1984: What Are the Differences and What Difference Does It Make?" (1985).

7. Lee, Sharon S. "The De-minoritization of Asian Americans: A Historical Examination of the Representations of Asian Americans in Affirmative Action Admissions Policies at the University of California." *Asian Am. LJ* 15 (2008): 129.

8. Turner, Wallace. "Rapid Rise in Students of Asian Origin Causing Problems at Berkeley Campus." *The New York Times*, April 9, 1981, 16.

9. Lee, Sharon S. "The De-minoritization of Asian Americans: A Historical Examination of the Representations of Asian Americans in Affirmative Action Admissions Policies at the University of California." *Asian Am. LJ* 15 (2008): 129.

10. Ibid.

11. Poon, OiYan A., and Megan S. Segoshi. "The Racial Mascot Speaks: A Critical Race Discourse Analysis of Asian Americans and *Fisher vs. University of Texas.*" *The Review of Higher Education* 42.1 (2018): 235–67.

12. Lee, Jennifer, Janelle Wong, Karthick Ramakrishnan, and Ryan Vinh. "69% of Asian American Registered Voters Support Affirmative Action." *Data Bits* (2022).

13. Lee, Jennifer. "Asian Americans, Affirmative Action & the Rise in Anti-Asian Hate." *Daedalus* 150.2 (2021): 180–98.

14. Lee, Jennifer, Janelle Wong, Karthick Ramakrishnan, and Ryan Vinh. "69% of Asian American Registered Voters Support Affirmative Action." *Data Bits* (2022).

15. Lee, Sharon S. "The De-minoritization of Asian Americans: A Historical Examination of the Representations of Asian Americans in Affirmative Action Admissions Policies at the University of California." *Asian Am. LJ* 15 (2008): 129.

16. Yoo, H. C., K. S. Burrola, and M. F. Steger. "A Preliminary Report on a New Measure: Internalization of the Model Minority Myth Measure (IM-4) and Its Psychological Correlates among Asian American College Students." *Journal of Counseling Psychology* 57 (2010): 114–27.

17. Bonacich, Edna. "A Theory of Middleman Minorities." *American Sociological Review* (1973): 583–94.

18. Matsuda, Mari. "We Will Not Be Used." *UCLA Asian Am. Pac. Is. LJ* 1 (1993): 79.

19. Omi, Michael, and Dana Y. Takagi. "Situating Asian Americans in the Political Discourse on Affirmative Action." *Representations* 55 (1996): 155–62.

20. Kim, Claire Jean. "The Racial Triangulation of Asian Americans." *Politics & Society* 27.1 (1999): 105–38.

21. Yi, Jacqueline, and Nathan R. Todd. "Internalized Model Minority Myth among Asian Americans: Links to Anti-Black Attitudes and Opposition to Affirmative Action." *Cultural Diversity and Ethnic Minority Psychology* 27.4 (2021): 569.

22. Poon, OiYan, Dian Squire, Corinne Kodama, Ajani Byrd, Jason Chan, Lester Manzano, Sara Furr, and Devita Bishundat. "A Critical Review of the Model Minority Myth in Selected Literature on Asian Americans and Pacific Islanders in Higher Education." *Review of Educational Research* 86.2 (2016): 469–502.

23. Chen, G. A., P. LePhuoc, M. R. Guzman, S. S. Rude, and B. G. Dodd, B. G. "Exploring Asian American Racial Ideology." *Cultural Diversity & Ethnic Minority Psychology* 12 (2006): 461–76.

24. Poon, OiYan A., and Megan S. Segoshi. "The Racial Mascot Speaks: A Critical Race Discourse Analysis of Asian Americans and *Fisher vs. University of Texas.*" *The Review of Higher Education* 42.1 (2018): 235–67.

25. Park, Julie J., and Amy Liu. "Interest Convergence or Divergence?: A Critical Race Analysis of Asian Americans, Meritocracy, and Critical Mass in the Affirmative Action Debate." *The Journal of Higher Education* 85.1 (2014): 36–64.

26. Perez, Michael P. "Pacific Identities Beyond US Racial Formations: The Case of Chamorro Ambivalence and Flux." *Social Identities* 8.3 (2002): 457–79.

27. Park, Julie J., and Amy Liu. "Interest Convergence or Divergence?: A Critical Race Analysis of Asian Americans, Meritocracy, and Critical Mass in the Affirmative Action Debate." *The Journal of Higher Education* 85.1 (2014): 36–64.

28. "Monitoring Student Growth." North Thurston Public Schools. November 16, 2020. Archived by Internet Archive Wayback Machine, https://web.archive.org/web/20201116053140if_/https: /www.nthurston.k12.wa.us/cms/lib/WA01001371/Centricity /Domain/2664/MonitoringStudentGrowth.pdf.

29. Leong, Kristen. "Whitewashing of Asian Students and a Report That Launched a Reckoning." KUOW NPR Network. February 5, 2021, https://www.kuow.org/stories/whitewashing-of-asian-students -and-the-report-that-launched-a-reckoning.

30. "Suicide Data and Statistics." Suicide Prevention. CDC. April 25, 2024, https://www.cdc.gov/suicide/suicide-data-statistics.html.

3 | Church Camp

1. Jeung, Russell. "Asian American Pan-Ethnic Formation and Congregational Culture." *Religions in Asian America: Building Faith Communities* 8 (2002): 215.

2. Lum, Kathryn Gin. *Heathen: Religion and Race in American History.* Harvard University Press, 2022.

3. Snow, Jennifer C. *A Border Made of Righteousness: Protestant Missionaries, Asian Immigration, and Ideologies of Race, 1850–1924.* Columbia University, 2003.

4. Seager, Robert. "Some Denominational Reactions to Chinese Immigration to California, 1856–1892." *Pacific Historical Review* 28.1 (1959): 49–66.

5. "Our History." First Chinese Baptist Church. Accessed April 30, 2024, https://www.fcbc.org/our-history/#:~:text=In%201952%2C%20we%20held%20our,and%20started%20the%20Crenshaw%20Mission.

6. Du Bois, William Edward Burghardt. *The Philadelphia Negro: A Social Study.* University of Pennsylvania Press, 1899.

7. Tomasi, Silvano M., and Madeline H. Engel. "The Italian Experience in the United States." (1970).

8. Tseng, Timothy. "Protestantism in Twentieth-Century Chinese America: The Impact of Transnationalism on the Chinese Diaspora." *Journal of American-East Asian Relations* 13.1–2 (2006): 121–48.

9. Hurh, Won Moo, and Kwang Chung Kim. "Religious Participation of Korean Immigrants in the United States." *Journal for the Scientific Study of Religion* (1990): 19–34.

10. Yang, Fenggang. "Chinese Conversion to Evangelical Christianity: The Importance of Social and Cultural Contexts." *Sociology of Religion* 59 (1998): 237–57.

11. Min, Pyong Gap, and Jung Ha Kim. *Religions in Asian America: Building Faith Communities.* AltaMira Press, 2001.

12. Wong, Janelle. "Race, Evangelicals and Immigration." *The Forum* 17.3 (2019): 403–19.

13. Tseng, Timothy. "The Changing Face of Evangelicalism." In C. G. Brown and M. Silk, eds. *The Future of Evangelicalism in America.* New York: Columbia University Press, 2016.

14. Hurh, W. M., and K. C. Kim. "Religious Participation of Korean Immigrants in the United States." *Journal for the Scientific Study of Religion* 29.1 (1990): 19–34.

15. Hong, Jane H. "In Search of a History of Asian American Evangelicals." *Religion Compass* 13.11 (2019): e12347.

16. Pew. "Asian Americans: A Mosaic of Faiths." Pew Research Center. July 19, 2012, https://www.pewforum.org/2012/07/19/asian-americans -a-mosaic-of-faiths-overview/.

17. Alumkal, Antony. "Scandal of the Model Minority Mind?: The Bible and Second-Generation Asian American Evangelicals." (2000).

18. Yang, Fenggang. "Chinese Conversion to Evangelical Christianity: The Importance of Social and Cultural Contexts." *Sociology of Religion* 59.3 (1998): 237–57.

19. Tseng, Timothy. "The Changing Face of Evangelicalism." In C. G. Brown and M. Silk, eds. *The Future of Evangelicalism in America.* New York: Columbia University Press, 2016.

20. Zylstra, S. E. "How the Second Generation of Korean-American Presbyterians Are Bridging the Gap." The Gospel Coalition (website), 2017.

21. Pew. "Asian Americans: A Mosaic of Faiths." Pew Research Center. July 19, 2012, https://www.pewforum.org/2012/07/19/asian-americans -a-mosaic-of-faiths-overview.

22. Hong, Jane H. "In Search of a History of Asian American Evangelicals." *Religion Compass* 13.11 (2019): e12347.

23. Park, Jerry Z., Joyce C. Chang, and James C. Davidson. "Equal Opportunity Beliefs beyond Black and White American Christianity." *Religions* 11.7 (2020): 348.

24. Wong, J., and J. Iwamura. "The Moral Minority: Race, Religion, and Conservative Politics in Asian America." In P. Hondagneu-Sotelo, ed. *Religion and Social Justice for Immigrants.* New Brunswick, NJ: Rutgers University Press, 2006.

25. Wong, Janelle, Kathy Rim, and Haven Perez. "Protestant Churches and Conservative Politics: Latinos and Asians in the United States." *Civic Hopes and Political Realities: Immigrants, Community Organizations, and Political Engagement* (2008): 271–99.

26. Wong, J. S. *Immigrants, Evangelicals, and Politics in an Era of Demographic Change.* New York: Russell Sage Foundation, 2018.

27. Park, Jerry Z., Joyce C. Chang, and James C. Davidson. "Equal Opportunity Beliefs beyond Black and White American Christianity." *Religions* 11.7 (2020): 348.

28. Palinkas, Lawrence A. *Rhetoric and Religious Experience: The Discourse of Immigrant Chinese Churches.* George Mason University Press, 1989.

29. Kwok, Pui-lan. "Asian and Asian American Churches." *Homosexuality and Religion: An Encyclopedia*, 59–62. Westport, CT: Greenwood Publishing Group, Inc., 2007.

30. Ibid.

31. Ibid.

32. Mohamed, Besheer, and Michael Rotolo. "Religion among Asian Americans." Pew Research Center. October 11, 2023, https://www.pewresearch.org/religion/2023/10/11/religion-among-asian-americans/.

33. "Black, Gay Communities Collide Over Gay Marriage." News and Notes NPR. November 13, 2008, https://www.npr.org/2008/11/13/96963827/black-gay-communities-collide-over-gay-marriage.

34. "Press Release: Data Showing That Asian American Voting on Prop 8 Significanty Influenced by Age, English Proficiency and Religiosity." NAKASEC. January 22, 2009, https://nakasec.org/1278.

35. Emerson, Michael O., and Christian Smith. *Divided by Faith: Evangelical Religion and the Problem of Race in America.* Oxford University Press, 2001.

36. Oyakawa, Michelle. "Racial Reconciliation as a Suppressive Frame in Evangelical Multiracial Churches." *Sociology of Religion* 80.4 (2019): 496–517.

37. Alumkal, Antony W. "American Evangelicalism in the Post–Civil Rights Era: A Racial Formation Theory Analysis." *Sociology of Religion* 65.3 (2004): 195–213.

38. Park, Jerry Z., Joyce C. Chang, and James C. Davidson. "Equal Opportunity Beliefs beyond Black and White American Christianity." *Religions* 11.7 (2020): 348.

39. Cheng, Patrick S. "Multiplicity and Judges 19: Constructing a Queer Asian Pacific American Biblical Hermeneutic." *Semeia: The Bible in Asian America* 90/91 (2002): 119–33.

4 | Racially Nowhere and Everywhere

1. Noah Arroyo, Mike Baker, Justin George, and Richard A. Oppel Jr. "Michael Brown: A Body's Timeline, 4 Hours on a Ferguson Street." *The New York Times*, August 23, 2014, https://www.nytimes.com/2014/08/24/us/michael-brown-a-bodys-timeline-4-hours-on-a-ferguson-street.html.

2. Sexton, Jared. "People-of-Color-Blindness: Notes on the Afterlife of Slavery." *Social Text* 28, no. 2 (2010): 31–56.

3. Garza, Alicia. "A Herstory of the #BlackLivesMatter Movement." *The Feminist Wire*, October 7, 2014.

4. Yellow Horse, Aggie J., Karen Kuo, Eleanor K. Seaton, and Edward D. Vargas. "Asian Americans' Indifference to Black Lives Matter: The Role of Nativity, Belonging and Acknowledgment of Anti-Black Racism." *Social Sciences* 10, no. 5 (2021): 168.

5. May, Vanessa. "Self, Belonging and Social Change." *Sociology* 45, no. 3 (2011): 363–78.

6. Bottero, Wendy. "Intersubjectivity and Bourdieusian Approaches to 'Identity.'" *Cultural Sociology* 4, no. 1 (2010): 3–22.

7. Wong, Janelle, S. Karthick Ramakrishnan, Taeku Lee, and Jane Junn. *Asian American Political Participation: Emerging Constituents and Their Political Identities*. New York: Russell Sage Foundation, 2011.

8. Liu, Wen. "Complicity and Resistance: Asian American Body Politics in Black Lives Matter." *Journal of Asian American Studies* 21 (2018): 421–51.

9. Ibid.

10. Yellow Horse, Aggie J., Karen Kuo, Eleanor K. Seaton, and Edward D. Vargas. "Asian Americans' Indifference to Black Lives Matter: The Role of Nativity, Belonging and Acknowledgment of Anti-Black Racism." *Social Sciences* 10, no. 5 (2021): 168.

11. Kendi, Ibram X. *How to Be an Antiracist*. New York: Random House, 2019.

12. Wang, Hansi Lo. "Awoken by N.Y.C. Cop Shooting, Asian-American Activists Chart Way Forward." NPR, April 23, 2016, https://www .npr.org/sections/codeswitch/2016/04/23/475369524/awoken-by -n-y-cop-shooting-asian-american-activists-chart-way-forward.

13. Liu, Wen. "Complicity and Resistance: Asian American Body Politics in Black Lives Matter." *Journal of Asian American Studies* 21 (2018): 421–51.

14. Kim, Nadia. "Asian Americans' Experiences of 'Race' and Racism." In *Handbooks of the Sociology of Racial and Ethnic Relations*. Edited by Hernán Vera and Joe R. Feagin. New York: Springer, 2007, 131–44.

15. Shange, Savannah, and Roseann Liu. "Solidarity as Debt: Fugitive Publics and the Ethics of Multiracial Coalition." Theorizing the Contemporary, Society for Cultural Anthropology (website), July 31, 2019, https://culanth.org/fieldsights/solidarity-as-debt -fugitive-publics-and-the-ethics-of-multiracial-coalition.

16. Wong, Janelle, S. Karthick Ramakrishnan, Taeku Lee, and Jane Junn. *Asian American Political Participation: Emerging Constituents and Their Political Identities*. New York: Russell Sage Foundation, 2011.

17. Arora, Maneesh, and Christopher T. Stout. "Letters for Black Lives: Co-ethnic Mobilization and Support for the Black Lives Matter Movement." *Political Research Quarterly* 72, no. 2 (2019): 389–402.

18. Lee, Helen, Quinmill Lei, Grace Su, and Sara Zhang. "Acknowledging Anti-Blackness, Overlooking Anti-Asian Racism: Missed Developmental Opportunities for Chinese American Youth." *Journal of Research on Adolescence* 32, no. 3 (2022): 1064–82.

19. Wong, Janelle. "Review of National Anti-Asian Hate Incident Reporting/Data Collection Published over 2019–2021." June 7, 2021, https://docs.google.com/document/d/19llMUCDHX-hLKru -cnDCqoBirlpNgFo7W3f-qoJoko4/edit.

20. Borja, Melissa, and Jacob Gibson. "Virulent Hate: Anti-Asian Racism in 2020." *Virulent Hate*, May 17, 2021, https://virulenthate.org/wp -content/uploads/2021/05/Virulent-Hate-Anti-Asian-Racism-In -2020-5.17.21.pdf.

5 | Ethnic Studies Helps Us Breathe Again

1. Umemoto, Karen. "'On Strike!' San Francisco State College Strike, 1968–69: The Role of Asian American Students." *Amerasia Journal* 15, no. 1 (1989): 3–41.

2. Fanon, Frantz. *The Wretched of the Earth*. New York: Grove Press, 2005, 62.

3. Tintiangco-Cubales, Allyson, Rita Kohli, Jocyl Sacramento, Nick Henning, Ruchi Agarwal-Rangnath, and Christine Sleeter. "Toward an Ethnic Studies Pedagogy: Implications for K–12 Schools from the Research." *The Urban Review* 47 (2015): 104–25.

4. Ray, Victor. "A Theory of Racialized Organizations." *American Sociological Review* 84, no. 1 (2019): 26–53.

5. Omi, Michael, and Howard Winant. *Racial Formation in the United States*. Routledge, 2014.

6. Yemenidjian, Natalie. "San Francisco State's Historic Ethnic Studies College May Have to Cut Courses, Faculty." KQED, April 20, 2024, https://www.kqed.org/news/10871294/s-f-states-historic-ethnic-studies-college-may-have-to-cut-courses-faculty.

7. Deloso, Shannon. "Asian American Women Students' Negotiating Power in Academia." *Fight the Tower: Asian American Women Scholars' Resistance and Renewal in the Academy* (2019): 165.

8. Ayestas, J. "California State University Task Force Investigates Ethnic Studies Funding." *State Hornet*, February 25, 2014, https://statehornet.com/2014/02/california-state-university-task-force-investigates-ethnic-studies-funding/.

9. Peña, Lorgia García. *Community as Rebellion: A Syllabus for Surviving Academia as a Woman of Color*. Haymarket Books, 2022.

10. Tintiangco-Cubales, Allyson, Rita Kohli, Jocyl Sacramento, Nick Henning, Ruchi Agarwal-Rangnath, and Christine Sleeter. "Toward an Ethnic Studies Pedagogy: Implications for K–12 Schools from the Research." *The Urban Review* 47 (2015): 104–25.

11. Shively, L.A. "Pershing's Chinese Leave Mark on History." *San Antonio Express-News*, May 28, 2011, https://www.mysanantonio

.com/news/military/article/Pershing-s-Chinese-leave-mark-on
-history-1395648.php.

12. Tintiangco-Cubales, Allyson, Rita Kohli, Jocyl Sacramento, Nick
Henning, Ruchi Agarwal-Rangnath, and Christine Sleeter. "Toward an Ethnic Studies Pedagogy: Implications for K–12 Schools
from the Research." *The Urban Review* 47 (2015): 104–25.

13. Daus-Magbual, Roderick R. "Political, Emotional, Powerful: The
Transformative Influence of the Pin@y Educational Partnerships."
Unpublished doctoral dissertation. University of San Francisco,
2010.

14. Tintiangco-Cubales, Allyson. "Giving Birth to Alagaan Pedagogy
(Pedagogy of Care)." *Fight the Tower: Asian American Women
Scholars' Resistance and Renewal in the Academy* (2019): 350.

15. Sleeter, C. E. *The Academic and Social Value of Ethnic Studies: A
Research Review.* Washington, DC: National Education Association,
2011.

16. Cabrera, N. L., J. F. Milem, and R. W. Marx. "An Empirical Analysis
of the Effects of Mexican American Studies Participation on Student
Achievement within Tucson Unified School District." Report submitted June 20, 2012, to Willis D. Hawley, PhD., Special Master for
the Tucson Unified School District Desegregation Case. University
of Arizona, http://works.bepress.com/nolan_l_cabrera/17/#.UKQ.

17. Daus-Magbual, Arlene, and Levalasi Loi-On. "Fighting for Our
Existence: Talanoas of Survival and Resistance at San Francisco
State." *AAPI Nexus: Policy, Practice and Community* 19, no. 1–2 (2022).

18. Coloma, Roland Sintos, Betina Hsieh, OiYan Poon, Stephanie Chang,
Sung Yeon Choimorrow, Manjusha P. Kulkarni, Grace Meng, Leigh
Patel, and Allyson Tintiangco-Cubales. "Reckoning with Anti-Asian
Violence: Racial Grief, Visionary Organizing, and Educational
Responsibility." *Educational Studies* 57, no. 4 (2021): 378–94.

19. Daus-Magbual, Arlene, and Levalasi Loi-On. "Fighting for Our
Existence: Talanoas of Survival and Resistance at San Francisco
State." *AAPI Nexus: Policy, Practice and Community* 19, no. 1–2 (2022).

20. Chavira-Prado, Alicia. "Ni Eres Ni Te Pareces: Academia as Rapture
and Alienation." *Counterpoints* 65, 135–52.

21. Ibid.

22. Fanon, Frantz. *The Wretched of the Earth*. New York: Grove Press, 20045, 62.

6 | Revolutionary Spirituality

1. Desis Rising Up and Moving. "Four Levels of Solidarity." Movement Hub, https://movementhub.org/resource/four-levels-of-solidarity.

2. Bambara, Toni Cade, and Kay Bonetti. *Toni Cade Bambara Interview with Kay Bonetti*. American Audio Prose Library, 1982.

3. Kaba, Mariame. *We Do This 'Til We Free us: Abolitionist Organizing and Transforming Justice*. Vol. 1. Haymarket Books, 2021.

4. Ibid.

5. Boggs, Grace Lee, and Scott Kurashige. *The Next American Revolution: Sustainable Activism for the Twenty-First Century*. University of California Press, 2012.

7 | Asian Diaspora: Returning to Radical Consciousness

1. CAMLA. "Roots: Asian American Movements in Los Angeles, 1968–1980s." 2017.

2. Umemoto, Karen. "'On Strike!' San Francisco State College Strike, 1968–69: The Role of Asian American Students." *Amerasia Journal* 15, no. 1 (1989): 3–41.

3. Nagel, Joane. *Race, Ethnicity, and Sexuality: Intimate Intersections, Forbidden Frontiers*. Vol. 324. New York: Oxford University Press, 2003.

4. Wu, Judy Tzu-Chun. "Asian American Feminisms and Women of Color Feminisms: Radicalism, Liberalism, and Invisibility." *Asian American Feminisms and Women of Color Politics* (2018): 43–65.

5. Asian Women. Berkeley: Univeristy of California, Asian American Studies Center. 1971/1975.

6. Bae, Aaron Byungjoo. "'The Struggle for Freedom, Justice, and Equality Transcends Racial and National Boundaries': Anti-Imperialism, Multiracial Alliances, and the Free Huey Movement in the San Francisco Bay Area." *Pacific Historical Review* 86, no. 4 (2017): 691–722.

7. Prashad, Vijay. *The Darker Nations: A People's History of the Third World.* The New Press, 2007.

8. Bobby Seale, Alex Hing, Sadie Lum, and Irwin Lum, in discussion with the author, July 2009; Fred Ho, ed. *Legacy to Liberation: Politics and Culture of Revolutionary Asian Pacific America.* San Francisco: AK Press, 2000.

9. Lee, Pam Tau. "The Struggle to Abolish Environmental and Economic Racism: Asian Radical Imagining from the Homeland to the Front Line." *Contemporary Asian American Activism: Building Movements for Liberation* (2022): 278–302.

10. Ibid.

11. Teves, Stephanie Nohelani, and Maile Arvin. "Decolonizing API: Centering Indigenous Pacific Islander Feminism." *Asian American Feminisms and Women of Color Politics* (2018): 107–37.

12. Trask, Haunani-Kay. *From a Native Daughter: Colonialism and Sovereignty in Hawaii (Revised Edition).* University of Hawaii Press, 1999.

13. Fujikane, Candace, and Jonathan Y. Okamura. *Asian Settler Colonialism: From Local Governance to the Habits of Everyday Life in Hawai'i.* University of Hawaii Press, 2008.

14. Hong, Grace Kyungwon. *The Ruptures of American Capital: Women of Color Feminism and the Culture of Immigrant Labor.* University of Minnesota Press, 2006.

15. Chow, Rey. *Writing Diaspora: Tactics of Intervention in Contemporary Cultural Studies.* Vol. 785. Indiana University Press, 1993.

16. Kwok, Pui-lan. *Postcolonial Imagination and Feminist Theology.* Westminster John Knox Press, 2005.

17. *Edward Said on "Orientalism."* Executive producer and director: Sut Jhally. Producer and editor: Sanjay Talreja. Assistant editor: Jeremy Smith. Featuring an interview with Edward Said, professor, Columbia

University, and author of *Orientalism*. Introduced by Sut Jhally, University of Massachusetts-Amherst. *Media Education Foundation*, 19.

18. Kwok, Pui-lan. *Postcolonial Imagination and Feminist Theology*. Westminster John Knox Press, 2005.

19. Jung, Moon-Ho. *Menace to Empire: Anticolonial Solidarities and the Transpacific Origins of the US Security State*. Vol. 63. University of California Press, 2022.

20. Ibid.

21. Ibid.

22. "Biography." Amado Khaya Initiative (website). Accessed May 8, 2024, https://amadokhaya.org/about.

23. Rodriguez, Robyn. "Amado Khaya Canham Rodriguez." Dr. Robyn Magalit Rodriguez (website). Accessed May 8, 2024, https://www.drrobynrodriguez.com/amadokhaya.

24. Compoc, Kim, Kathleen Aspillaga Corpuz, and Vernadette Vicuña Gonzalez. "A Filipinx Settler Ally Manifesto." *Closer to Liberation: Pin[a/x]y Activism in Theory and Practice* (2023): 171–84.

About the Author

BIANCA MABUTE-LOUIE is a scholar/activist completing her PhD in sociology at Rice University, where she researches the intersections of race, religion, and politics. She is published in top academic journals, including *Social Forces* and *Sociology of Race and Ethnicity*, as well as in public outlets like *Elle* magazine. Bianca's work has been featured on CNN and ABC and in *Time* and the *LA Times*, among other outlets. Over the last decade, Bianca has served Asian American community organizations and taught Asian American Studies. She currently sits on the board of Asian Texans for Justice. Through her work in academia and in the community, Bianca is committed to the praxis of solidarity and collective liberation.